ADAM HAMILTON

Unleashing the Word

Preaching with Relevance,
Purpose, and Passion

Abingdon Press
Nashville

UNLEASHING THE WORD
PREACHING WITH RELEVANCE, PURPOSE, AND PASSION

This book is printed on recycled, acid-free paper.

Library of Congress Cataloging-in-Publication Data

Hamilton, Adam, 1964-
  Unleashing the word : preaching with relevance, purpose, and passion /
Adam Hamilton.
    p. cm.
  ISBN 0-687-08315-X (alk. paper)
  1. Preaching. I. Title.

  BV4211.3.H36 2003
  251--dc21

                                                                2003008058

Scripture quotations are from The New Revised Standard Version of the Bible, copyright © 1989, by the Division of Christian Education of the National Council of the Churches of Christ in the United States of America. Used by permission

The material on the enclosed DVD is copyright © Church of the Resurrection. All materials on the DVD are written by Adam Hamilton, except the video entitled "How Far Can We See," which was written and produced by Constance E. Stella.

03 04 05 06 07 08 09 10 11 12 — 10 9 8 7 6 5 4 3 2 1

MANUFACTURED IN THE UNITED STATES OF AMERICA

*With grateful appreciation
to the Reverend Ray Firestone,
pastor, friend, mentor—
for your encouragement and wisdom,
which have been invaluable to me*

Let the elders who rule well be considered worthy of double honor, especially those who labor in preaching and teaching.

—*1 Timothy 5:17*

CONTENTS

INTRODUCTION

So you are a preacher—or you hope to become one. Good! The world needs preachers. Isaiah, Israel's greatest prophet and preacher, captured it well when he said,

How beautiful upon the mountains
   are the feet of the messenger who announces peace,
who brings good news,
   who announces salvation,
   who says to Zion, "Your God reigns." (Isaiah 52:7)

And the apostle Paul, who preached the gospel throughout the Roman Empire, quotes Isaiah in Romans 10:13-14:

"Everyone who calls on the name of the Lord shall be saved." But how are they to call on one in whom they have not believed? And how are they to believe in one of whom they have never heard? And how are they to hear without someone to proclaim him?

Clearly, preaching is important.

Yet we live in a day and time where "preaching" and "sermons" are often used to describe things we don't like. We don't want our parents to "preach" to us. We don't need another "sermon" from those who try to correct us. Some have said the very idea of preaching, the kind that is done in churches, is ridiculous in our new "post-Christian," multimedia, entertainment-oriented information age. Others simply point to the diminishing role of the church in society, and the clergy scandals from the left and the right, noting that the days when preachers influenced society and shaped our culture are over.

I believe such pronouncements are premature. In fact, the need for effective preaching has never been greater. We live in a time when people are searching for meaning, looking for hope and good news, and genuinely want to hear a word from God. The events we watch unfold on the evening news—snipers killing innocent people, terrorist cells looking for their next target; as well as the struggles we face in daily living—physical illness, aging, loneliness, and problems with our relationships—all leave us hungry for help, hope, and answers. And despite our doubts, most people still long to believe in God, and they are hopeful that God has a plan for their lives and answers to their struggles and questions.

For these reasons I am persuaded that there is a great need and desire for effective preaching today—and those who learn how to effectively preach to twenty-first-century people have the potential to significantly influence the lives of their hearers, and through them the culture in which they live. Your preaching can transform people's lives, change the culture, and renew your church. In fact, it may very well be that no one has a greater potential to bring hope, healing, and light to your community than you.

Effective preaching begins with your conviction that what you do when you preach is important. If you don't believe that, you might as well put this book down—there is no reason to go on until you've found this conviction. But if you believe that God can use you and your preaching as a vehicle for personal and social transformation, if you believe that your preaching really matters, this book was written for you—with the hope of offering insights, suggestions, and ideas that may help your preaching be as effective as possible.

CHAPTER ONE

PREACHING WITH PURPOSE

For the next few hours (if you actually read this entire book in one sitting) we're going to spend time together, and I will be sharing with you what I hope will be at least a few great ideas for sermons, a host of insights that will rouse your own creativity, and some concrete hints that may improve your effectiveness in preaching.

What I share with you comes not from what I have read in a textbook, though I have read numerous books on preaching, and I am sure they have shaped my preaching in many ways. Nor does what I will share with you come from my seminary courses on preaching, though I had several excellent preaching professors who, I am sure, influenced my preaching more than I even realize. What I share with you comes from getting up week after week and preaching, six times per weekend, to a congregation of wonderful, and by and large highly educated, people, most of whom were relatively unchurched prior to joining the church I serve. It comes from working with the group of incredibly gifted folks on our worship planning team, who together help me to constantly refine and improve both the sermon planning process and the actual writing and preaching of the sermons themselves. It comes from preaching hundreds of weddings and funerals over the years, and watching as a significant number of people actually joined the church as a result of the ministry provided at those times. And it comes from listening to people as they share with me what speaks to them, and sometimes what frustrates them, from the sermons I have preached.

Before we jump into specific techniques and ideas related to preaching, it seems appropriate to begin by laying out my thoughts on what preaching is supposed to be.

What Is Preaching Supposed to *Be*?

I understand that in preaching we are assuming the terrifying responsibility of speaking on behalf of God. This should be a frightening proposition—one misstep and we find ourselves violating the third commandment by misusing the name of the Lord, while misleading or potentially damaging our hearers.

Fortunately we are not left to our own thoughts when it comes to trying to discern what God's word is for our congregation. We have a starting point—the Scriptures. We believe that in and through the Bible God offers us a timeless word for our lives and for our world today. Paul, writing to Timothy as he gave oversight to the church at Ephesus, offered this important reminder:

> But as for you, continue in what you have learned and firmly believed, knowing from whom you learned it, and how from childhood you have known the sacred writings that are able to instruct you for salvation through faith in Christ Jesus. All scripture is inspired by God and is useful for teaching, for reproof, for correction, and for training in righteousness, so that everyone who belongs to God may be proficient, equipped for every good work. (2 Timothy 3:14-17)

Effective preaching begins, then, with effective listening. My wife, LaVon, is a sign language interpreter at a local community college. She interprets the instructors' lectures so that students who are deaf and hearing-impaired can take these courses. In order to do her job properly, she has to listen very, very carefully to the instructor. If she misses a word, or fails to understand a concept, she cannot properly pass on the idea to her students. She knows that these students don't come to class to hear what she knows about math or English or art. They come grateful for her willingness to use her skills to help them hear what the instructor has to say on these topics.

In the same way, we who are preachers are charged with listening very carefully for what God would say to his people. Unfortunately God does not dictate our sermons to us. In order to hear this word we must study carefully what God has already said through the Scriptures. We are the interpreters, and our parishioners come not to hear what we know about any given topic, but to have us use our skills and training to interpret and translate what God would say to them, in a way that they can understand and apply to their lives.

What Is Preaching Supposed to *Do*?

If this is what preaching is supposed to be, what is preaching supposed to *do*? In other words, what is its purpose?

I probably missed this lecture in seminary, and I am even a little embarrassed to admit what I am about to tell you. But after two degrees in theology and ministry, and multiple preaching classes; after reading some of the best books published on preaching, and after having preached hundreds of sermons, I had never stopped to think about what I was supposed to be doing when I preached.

Don't get me wrong. I knew I was supposed to do my homework—carefully exegeting the biblical text, praying about the implications of that text for my hearers, inviting God to speak to and through me, searching for a handful of good illustrations, and then delivering the sermon with enough passion, conviction, and clarity that people would be moved. I understood all of this. But

I had not stopped to think about the goals or aims of my preaching.

I suppose if someone asked me what the goal of my preaching was, I would have come up with an answer. But it was several years into preaching on a weekly basis before I realized that I needed to gain some clarity on why I was going through this exercise each week. What triggered this, I suppose, was the need I felt to clarify the purpose of the church itself. Why did this church that I was pastoring exist? What was its purpose? What were we trying to accomplish here?

Ultimately we drafted a purpose statement for our congregation that reads, "The purpose of the United Methodist Church of the Resurrection is to build a Christian community where nonreligious and nominally religious people are becoming deeply committed Christians." I shared with our people that everything we do as a church should somehow tie back in to that purpose statement. Every ministry, every program, every service should be designed to help us accomplish the mission outlined in this purpose statement. (Though this realization and the development of our purpose statement came some time before I had heard of the Saddleback Church in southern California, and before the publication of Rick Warren's excellent book *The Purpose-Driven Church*, I am not sure anyone has summarized these ideas better than Warren has.)

It was then that I realized my preaching was no different from any other avenue of the church's ministry. And I began to understand that the purpose of my preaching each week is to do everything a sermon can do to "build a Christian community where nonreligious and nominally religious people are becoming deeply committed Christians."

I took this one step farther and asked, "What does a deeply committed Christian look like, and what role might my preaching play in helping develop this kind of person?" To answer the first part of this question Methodists have, for over two hundred years, looked to Jesus, who taught that we are to "love God with all your heart, soul, and mind" and "love your neighbor as you love yourself." We describe these two as personal piety and social holiness. John Wesley, the eighteenth-century founder of Methodism, used one word to describe the end or goal of the Christian life: *sanctification*. With these ideas in mind, I was gaining clarity around my purpose in preaching. It was (1) to help foster and build authentic Christian community where Christians learn to minister to one another and develop healthy, caring relationships; (2) to attract unchurched and nominally churched people; and (3) to help my hearers come to love God with their intellect and their heart and to reflect that love in their actions toward others.

Accomplishing the Aims of Preaching

As with most successful ventures, I believe effective preaching must start with the end in mind, and then a plan must be developed to accomplish that end.

This, however, is not how I thought of preaching prior to this time. My sermons, up to 1992, were derived from texts assigned by the Revised Common Lectionary—a set of scripture readings for each weekend of the year using a three-year cycle. Each week I would choose one of four preassigned texts, and away I'd go. I had no overall plan for what I hoped to accomplish by my preaching over time. No sense of trying to balance out certain kinds of preaching with other kinds. It was simply a week-to-week effort of preaching the best sermon I could from the assigned text. (I find that many pastors who come from traditions that do not use the Lectionary nevertheless prepare sermons in a similar way. They choose scriptures to preach on, or topical themes that seem interesting, but without a thought to how a year's worth of sermons may work together to accomplish a clearly stated goal.)

Imagine with me a carpenter going to a job site each week, finding plenty of wood and nails, and then working on building whatever he or she got excited about building that week. The carpenter might decide one week he wanted to build cabinets. The next week he was excited about building garage doors. The next week it might be pouring concrete. No one hoping to build a house would work that way. No, if you want to build a house you must develop a set of plans, put together a construction timeline, and then work this plan step-by-step so that each part of the house is built in its proper order until the plans are fulfilled.

Again, I am embarrassed to admit that I prepared my sermons, week after week, in this way. But there it is. You have probably already thought through this issue, and you may already have a picture in mind of what you hope the people in your congregation will know, become, and do as a result of your preaching in the next year or two. You may have carefully thought through what it looks like to become a committed Christian and what kind of sermons it would take for this to happen. If so, I commend you. But if not, you are in good company. Most pastors I know have not looked at their preaching in this way.

Here's what happened once I started looking at the purpose of my preaching. I began to see that there were really at least five things my sermons needed to accomplish across the course of a year, in order to have a reasonable chance of fulfilling the church's purpose of building Christian community, helping to reach nonreligious and nominally religious people, and moving all our members toward becoming deeply committed Christians:

1. Evangelism
2. Discipleship
3. Pastoral Care
4. Equipping and Sending
5. Institutional Development

To borrow the home-building metaphor once again, each of these five represents a different specialty—a different part of the construction process. Evangelism may be the foundation; Discipleship the framing of the home; Pastoral Care may be the roof, heating, electrical, and plumbing systems; Equipping and Sending the finish work—paint, carpet, and trim that makes the house complete; and Institutional Development might be the upkeep and maintenance required to keep the house in good condition.

Once I gained some clarity on the importance of these various types of sermons or, better, of these various aims to be accomplished by my preaching, I needed to develop a plan to accomplish them.

CHAPTER TWO

DEVELOPING A PREACHING PLAN

I have mentioned already the Revised Common Lectionary—a wonderful tool to help churches read through the Bible over the course of three years. I was taught in seminary that faithful preachers would "stick with the Lectionary." I was taught that if one didn't preach by the Lectionary, the pastor would be in danger of forever returning to his or her favorite biblical stories, and he or she would avoid preaching on difficult texts. Somewhere along the way I was also told that effective preaching always started with the text of the Bible, and never with a topic of one sort or another.

There is much to be said for preaching according to the Lectionary cycle. But when I began to look at my preaching in the light of the larger purpose of the church, and I began to try to map out a plan for how to accomplish that purpose over the course of a year or two, the use of the Lectionary became frustrating. In some ways, using the Lectionary to build this house—to accomplish the five aims and the purpose of the church—was like a lumberyard delivering a load of wonderful building supplies to a job site without ever seeing a copy of the building plans or knowing what size, shape, or design the house was meant to be. It might be possible to build the house according to the plans with the supplies that were delivered, but it would be a very tedious, frustrating, and infinitely more difficult process.

So in 1992 I let go of my need to use the Lectionary. I return to the Lectionary during the season of Advent most years. But since 1992 my messages throughout the rest of the year have been preached as part of a sermon series strategically designed to accomplish one or more of the aims I have mentioned.

This, however, was only the first step in creating a preaching plan. In this chapter I would like to describe the process by which I outline sermon themes twenty-four months in advance.

As I hinted at in the last chapter, in the early 1990s my preaching plan looked something like this: On Monday morning I would read the four preassigned Lectionary passages, choose one that seemed most to speak to our church's situation, and begin researching this passage. By Thursday I would have completed my first draft of the manuscript and be able to put together the rest of the service, choosing hymns, prayers, and other acts of worship to tie in to the sermon theme. What was lacking in this approach was the opportunity for the choir to prepare an anthem that would be linked to the sermon (choral music needs to be ordered at least six weeks in advance and then rehearsed). There was no opportunity for the choir or instrumentalists to rehearse the hymns so they could be effective song leaders (rehearsal was on Wednesday night). We did not use video at the time, but had we been doing so, it would have been impossible to develop excellent video support for the sermon twenty-four hours before the first worship service. And there was no opportunity for any other ministry areas, especially our discipleship and education ministries, to tie in to the worship themes.

Today I have sermon series outlines for the next two years. Those for the next twelve months have dates, titles, and basic ideas for each sermon. The sermons coming up in the next two series have detailed outlines with major themes. Our staff have access to these themes and are encouraged to plan to tie in to these themes wherever possible. Our video and music teams are able to discuss ideas for songs and video to support the sermons months in advance. We have, on occasion, tied in major musical presentations to the sermon themes. Several years ago I preached a series of sermons on Joseph, the son of Jacob. Our music ministry produced *Joseph and the Amazing Technicolor Dreamcoat* to coincide with this series. The following year I preached a series of sermons on Elijah, and the music ministry produced Mendelssohn's masterpiece oratorio *Elijah*. In both cases the sermon helped make the music ministry performance a success and the performance helped make the sermon series a success. In addition, in each worship service, preludes, hymns, praise songs, pastoral prayers, anthems, and offertories all work together to support a common theme. On occasion I will include references back to the anthem (which precedes the sermon) during the message.

As you read the examples of various sermon series that I will mention in later chapters, keep in mind the process described in this chapter. Exceptional sermon series, those that make use of video and the arts, provide opportunities for other ministry areas to "piggyback" on the themes by starting studies or launching new ministries, and those that provide service response opportunities, happen only when everyone has time to plan and work together.

If I were reading this chapter ten years ago, I would say that this idea of planning sermons two years in advance is impossible. I would also have raised the question of how a pastor can respond to the immediate issues of the time when sermons have been planned out two years in advance. Allow me to focus on this second issue first.

While sermons are planned out two years in advance, there is generally at least one sermon series, or part of a series, that we end up changing each year. Sometimes the series no longer seems appropriate. Sometimes it is dismissed as I try to develop more detail and find it simply doesn't fit the needs of the congregation at the time. Our aim is to make these changes several months in advance, giving our other ministries enough time to adjust. This doesn't happen often, but it does happen. In addition, when there are major events that take place in our country or in our congregation, our staff and congregation know we will drop what we had planned to address the current need. The strongest example of this was the terrorist attacks of September 11, 2001. We postponed the sermons we had planned for three weeks to focus on the pastoral care needs of the community and our congregation.

Even with a sermon plan that stretches out two years into the future, each sermon is an opportunity to focus on the issues of the day. An example is a series of sermons I preached in the fall of 2002 on the letters of Paul. Each week we examined a different epistle, spending the first third of the sermon teaching about the historical background and setting of the letter. The rest of the sermon examined one or two key ideas from the epistle. I had chosen the key ideas from each epistle six months in advance, but even so, each week as I prepared the sermon I would find that at least one of the points of the sermon would change from my earlier outline based on the events unfolding in our nation or the needs of our congregation.

But how does a preacher go from developing sermons on a weekly, or even monthly basis, to developing two years' worth of sermon ideas? That will be the focus of the rest of this chapter.

Developing a Long-Term Preaching Plan

There are three things that are essential to developing a long-term preaching plan:

1. Time away.
2. An awareness of the needs of your congregation and the issues facing the community and world.
3. Prayer.

Time Away

Let's begin with time. It is impossible to develop a preaching plan, even for several months out, without having adequate time away from the day-to-day pastoral activities of the church. You must have time to pray, to reflect, to read, and to outline—all without distractions. I cannot do this at home. I have to get away to a retreat center to do this. This is not vacation time. It is not continuing education. It is a part of your legitimate workload if you are going to be an effective parish preacher. During this time it is important that your congregation understands what you are doing, why, and what value this brings to them and to the quality of your preaching. If you are in a small church, it is important that you have laypeople who can cover your pastoral responsibilities in your absence.

My time away for outlining and planning sermons looks like this: I take two weeks off every July as a "study leave." At least part of this time is spent completely on my own at a retreat center, while part of it may be spent working in my home study or the local seminary library while still spending the evenings with my wife and children. During this two weeks I will spend roughly ninety hours reading, praying, writing, and outlining sermons. This last summer, when I was finished with this ninety hours I brought back to our staff enough sermon series ideas to last four years, inviting them to pray and give me feedback on which ideas spoke most clearly to them or seemed most needful for our church. In addition, I came back with detailed outlines for the upcoming three months of sermons, and a bit more information about themes and ideas for the nine months of sermons following that. I'll tell you more about what I specifically do to generate these ideas below. Is this two weeks beneficial to the church? Absolutely. And in the process, it is renewing to me!

In addition to this time in July, I will take two days off just after the Christmas holiday to update the sermon plan and do additional research on the upcoming sermons. Finally, twice each year I will take the weekend off from worship and use the two days in which I would have prepared sermons for that weekend to go away once more to read, pray, and outline sermons. This gives me a total of fifteen days of sermon outlining and planning each year. This time improves the quality of the preaching and worship at our church and pays off many times over.

Allow me to tell you a little more of what I do while I am away on a typical two- or three-day study retreat. I have taken these planning retreats at Methodist camps, our members' vacation homes, a Roman Catholic monastery, and sometimes at my house when my wife and children have gone to visit family out of town. The key thing for me is to minimize distractions. I also find that I pray better when I can walk through the woods; my creativity is opened when I am outdoors.

Prayer and Awareness of Current Needs

I come to these retreats with a set of questions: Where are the people in my church hurting? What are they afraid of or concerned about? Where are they in their faith? Where do they most need to grow? What are the portions of scripture or theological, pastoral, or spiritual subjects I have neglected in my preaching in the last year? How can I help my parishioners grow in their relationship with Christ? How can I help them more effectively live out their faith in the world? What are the needs of the church itself? And, what does God want to say to his children?

I will often write these questions out on a piece of paper and come back to them throughout the retreat. During this time away I will take a box of books, newspaper clippings, prayer request cards, a list of major events or initiatives of the church, my personal goals, and my Bible. I begin the time away by taking a long "prayer walk." I may walk for an hour singing hymns, praying, and worshiping God. My aim is to open myself wholly to the Holy Spirit. I ask God to guide me, to help me understand what to say to the congregation entrusted to my care. This time of prayer is renewing to me, and I usually come back to the room with my head filled with ideas and answers to the questions mentioned above. I may write a few of these down, but I will focus the next hour on reading from the Scriptures, looking over the goals we have set for the church for the coming year, scanning newspaper clippings to give me an idea of the issues facing our world, and then looking over the pages of prayer request cards that our congregants have turned in, praying over them and reflecting on what they tell me about the pastoral needs of our church.

Having spent time reflecting on these various sources of input, I will begin answering the questions I've mentioned above ("Where are the people hurting?" etc.) as ideas come to me. After a couple of hours I will go for another prayer walk, repeating this cycle of prayer, reflection, and writing multiple times throughout the retreat. This process will generally generate dozens of sermon series ideas—far more than I could use—so I file these ideas on my computer to bring up at future retreats. Some of the sermon ideas I have used in the last year were first generated four or five years ago on previous retreats.

Lay It Out

Next, I will diagram on a piece of paper the next two years, month my month. I will write down the things I know will be happening during various times in the year (for example, each fall we have a three-week emphasis on stewardship). Then I begin to lay out the five aims of my preaching described in chapter 2. Below is a sample of the types of sermons I will often focus on during the various parts of the year:

Jan.-Feb.	Lent	May-June	July-August	Sept.-Oct.	November	Advent
Evangelism	Discipleship	Pastoral Care	Discipleship	Equip/ Send	Institutional Development	Open

As we'll discuss in more detail in chapter 7, I plan sermons for January-February that will attract the multitude of visitors who come out for candlelight Christmas Eve services, motivating them to return. If we've done our job and kept them through February, then we move on to try to deepen their faith, and the faith of all our members, with a Lenten series that teaches on a section of scripture, spiritual disciplines, or some aspect of Christian theology. We will typically invite the entire congregation to read through one of the Gospels during the season of Lent as well (more on that in chapter 8, where we will look at the use of study guides that correspond to my sermons). Following Easter we will often focus on pastoral care sermons that will be attractive to Easter visitors and at the same time provide healing, hope, and comfort for our members. During July and August, when typically our most committed members are present each week, we will focus once more on discipleship, though often the sermons will be on a theme that we hope will encourage our members to attend worship. The early fall will generally include a sermon series that equips, inspires, and challenges people to go "higher up and farther in" as they seek to grow in their faith. We often will tie in "ministry fairs" where our worshipers can sign up for small groups or areas of service.

During these sermons I will remind the congregation of the membership expectations of our church. These expectations include: worshiping every weekend, and so we'll preach on the meaning and practice of worship; the intentional pursuit of spiritual growth through activity in a small group or other vehicle for growth, so we'll preach on the importance of small groups; serving God with one's time in at least one ministry area of the church each year, and so we'll preach on the call to serve; and giving financially in proportion to one's income with the tithe being the biblical challenge—we'll often wait to preach on this theme until November when we focus on our annual financial campaign. Finally, in December we will pick up Advent themes, preparing our members to celebrate Christ's birth. For these sermons I will usually return to the Lectionary, and then look for a creative and interesting way of approaching these scriptures (I'll share a few of our recent Advent series in chapter 11).

With this framework in mind, I will begin placing the sermon series ideas that have been generated during my time in prayer and reflection on this calendar. This becomes the basis for the sermon plan I will present to our worship planning team.

Generally I will devote half my time on these study leaves to generating future sermon ideas, and the other half will be spent reading, researching, and outlining the sermons that are coming up in the next few months to a year. For example, in the summer of 2002 I spent three days at a Benedictine monastery in complete silence. During this time I walked, prayed, and pursued the regimen I've described above. I spent one and a half days working on future sermon series ideas. The rest of the time I devoted to reading through the letters of Paul, outlining them, and studying materials related to them. This allowed me to return to our worship staff meeting the following Monday with detailed outlines of sermons for August to December, and paragraph summaries of sermons for January and February of the following year. Beyond this I had sermon series titles, summaries of the series with a breakdown of individual sermon topics, but no specific information on these sermons.

I've just attempted to describe in writing a process that I use to generate ideas and to outline sermons for up to two years in advance. As I reread it, it sounds more complicated than it really is. Here is the important point to remember: You can develop sermon plans for months, if not years, ahead, but it will require quality, uninterrupted time for you to pray, reflect upon the needs of your congregation, and picture what is necessary to help your congregation members become deeply committed Christians. You may want to start by planning twelve months in advance, or maybe just six months. If you try this I believe you will find that your preaching and worship will be more effective as your messages unfold to accomplish your ministry goals, enabling you to build a congregation of committed Christians.

Scripture Selection

One final word seems in order regarding topical or thematic preaching. As I have noted, some of the sermons I preach are expositions of biblical books or the texts related to certain biblical characters. But when I am preparing a sermon on a certain topic or theme—forgiveness, perhaps, or some dimension of marriage, how do I select the scriptures to focus on these messages without falling into the temptation to misuse a scripture or try to force a scripture to address a topic it wasn't originally aimed at addressing? There are several keys here. First, the more I study the Bible, the more familiar I become with its message, which makes it possible for the Holy Spirit to bring to mind a particular scripture I have studied in the past (see John 14:26). The second is that as I am studying a particular issue or topic carefully, I will also be looking to see what other Christians have said about this topic and where they have seen a connection between the Scriptures and this topic. Finally, and this is perhaps the most important, the search for the scriptures that address various issues or topics will require diligent research. I search the Scriptures using Bible software; I make use of the cross-references in my study Bibles, and I spend time striving to think creatively about what similar kinds of issues the biblical authors may have faced or addressed. Topical Bibles can help in this process as well. The key, of course, is to ensure that we are offering an authentic word from God, or expounding on a clear biblical principle that addresses the contemporary situation. Through adequate study, reading, and research, this is not only possible, but truly exciting.

Now that we've looked at developing plans, setting goals, and outlining sermons in advance, let's focus on the weekly task of preparing a sermon.

CHAPTER THREE

WRITING THE SERMON

Most of you reading this book have been writing sermons for years—some for far longer than I have. You likely have a style and a way of doing this that work well for you. I will take the time to describe my aim as I prepare each sermon, as well as the actual process I use to move from the outline (generated in the planning retreats I described in chapter 2) to the final draft as it is preached.

The Aim of the Sermon

First, a word about my aim in preaching preparation. Regardless of the subject matter, my aim is that every sermon I preach be the best-researched sermon our congregation will ever hear on this particular theme or passage of scripture. My sermon style is part teaching and part preaching. I hope that congregation members will learn at least one thing they didn't know before from every sermon (which means I likely need to learn more than one new thing as I prepare the sermon!). I also hope not simply to teach them, but to relate the Word of God, or the lesson from the scripture, in such a way that they see the relevance to their lives—that in some way they are encouraged, helped, blessed, or moved to action by the message. As a teacher my hope is that each sermon series would be equivalent to a college-level course (though abbreviated) on whatever the theme may be.

For example, in the series of sermons mentioned earlier titled "The Letters of Paul," my aim was that this series meet or exceed the quality of information and presentation of a similar course I took in college. By the time we were finished with this series, I wanted our congregation members to have a solid grasp of where each letter was sent and why Paul wrote it, how the New Testament was put together, and how the letters fit into the life of Paul outlined in the book of Acts. Each sermon included maps of the journeys of Paul and video and slides showing the ruins of the ancient cities to which Paul wrote. (In preparation for this series of sermons, I led a group of forty-three church members on a thirteen-day tour of the Second Missionary Journey of Paul, traveling through Greece and Turkey—a trip that had significant influence on my own understanding of Paul and his writings. This trip took a year to plan, and its coordination with the sermon series was possible only because I had a sermon plan generated two years in advance!)

Yet my aim in that sermon series was not simply to provide cognitive information about Paul and his letters, but to use this information to help worshipers hear the main themes from each letter and then to relate these themes to their daily lives. It is here that each message begins to look more like a traditional sermon.

So, what kind of preparation does it take to pull off a sermon like this? Allow me to walk through the typical preparation of these messages.

Preparing a Sermon

On Monday I arrive at the office about 9:45 A.M., taking the opportunity to rest in the morning following a weekend of worship services. I go to the sanctuary and begin in prayer. I will walk through each section of chairs, praying for those who will be in worship the coming weekend and asking God to prepare me to hear what he would say to them. After ten or fifteen minutes in prayer I head to our worship planning meeting. I will describe in more detail who is on this team and what happens at our meetings in chapter 6.

We begin this meeting with prayer, inviting God to guide us, use us, and minister through us. We pray that the worship we plan will be led by the Holy Spirit, will honor God, and will be a vehicle through which God can minister to his people. We typically meet for an hour and a half, with half of that time focused on the upcoming week's sermon, and the other half focused on future worship services, special worship services, or various ways we can improve what we are doing in worship. As it relates to the upcoming weeks' sermons, the worship planning team will look over, once again, the preaching plan I distributed months before. They will have already started preparing their various elements of worship according to this plan. I will walk them through the direction I am heading with the sermon, and invite their input or ideas—both for sermon content and for any other creative ideas for worship that weekend.

From here I head back to my study at home, where it is much quieter than the office, to do the preliminary work on my message. I typically have a stack of books and other resources I am using to research the particular sermon I am about to write. For a more detailed look at what happens next, let's examine the actual sermon preparation for a message I preached on Paul's letter to Titus as part of the series I've described above.

I began my work on the sermon at home in prayer, asking God to help me hear God's word and to grow in my own faith as I studied. Next, I copied and pasted the letter to Titus from my Bible software program into my word processor, where I read the letter carefully and typed in my own initial thoughts and commentary. As my next step, I read the introduction to this epistle from three different commentaries. Following this I performed a search in my Bible software program to find all the references to Titus in the New Testament (there were thirteen, most of which were in 2 Corinthians), and I began to outline everything that could be known with certainty about Titus from the New Testament. I then began to look for extrabiblical references to Titus from the patristic period by searching an electronic version of the work of the early church fathers that I have on CD-ROM. I also searched the Internet for information, discovering the purported site of Titus's burial on Crete and the information that he lived to be ninety-four. I went back and reread the epistle in the light of this information. I began looking for the underlying issues that prompted Paul to write this epistle and began noting these, cross-referencing what I was seeing with the commentaries.

From here I looked for connecting points between the emphases in Titus, specifically issues related to the organization of the early church and the expectations of leaders, and the concerns and issues in the life of the church I pastor. One of the major strategic goals for the coming year at our church was going to be an emphasis on small groups and the raising up of leaders, patterned after the elders of the Pastoral Epistles—thus I felt the Holy Spirit kindle an excitement about the possibility of casting this vision as we studied Titus. The major emphasis in Titus was the author's insistence that Titus challenge the Christians on Crete to pursue "good works"—to, in the words of Jesus, let their "light shine." I began to wonder how this challenge tied in to the launch of our stewardship emphasis for November, in which we were challenging people to take a broader look at stewardship—to see it as living fully committed lives—serving God with all that we are. Was there a connection between Paul's challenge for the Cretan Christians not to be "lazy" but to live their faith "out loud" and God's call on our members not to be content with a kind of "spectator" Christianity, but to take the next step in actively pursuing their service to God?

The Manuscript

The research and the initial direction I've described above represent approximately six hours of working, reading, and studying.

The next day, after once again praying and seeking God's direction, I would use the notes I had made to begin writing the first draft of the manuscript, pausing to read Titus one more time. By now I was getting genuinely excited about Titus and what I had learned about him, what I had been reminded of as a result of my study, and the insights I felt I was receiving for my own life. With my first draft of the manuscript finished, I could begin working on the sermon notes for the weekend's bulletin (more on the sermon notes and study guides in chapter 8).

This week, with Titus being a relatively short epistle, the initial work on my sermon was finished in about ten hours. From here I sat on the sermon for two days, occasionally coming back to look it over, or to reread Titus. During this time I gave our video team the photos of the ruins from Crete that we had found on the Internet, and the maps I wanted to use in the sermon. We considered other possible sermon illustrations or the use of a video interview, but for the most part I did not focus much attention on the sermon during these two days. By late Thursday evening I had reworked the manuscript of the sermon, creating a second draft, and then I developed a study guide for the letter. I e-mailed the manuscript to our video department on Friday so they could copy any scriptures I used in the sermon body itself into our computer program for use on the video screen as I preached.

On Saturday afternoon I rewrote the manuscript once again. This allowed me to strengthen the manuscript and transitions, and it also served to commit the text to memory. Generally I will have at least three and sometimes as many as six or seven drafts of each sermon manuscript—often the challenge is to shorten the sermons to fit into a thirty-three-minute time frame.

At 4:30 P.M. I printed off the final manuscript and made copies for our video department and for several hearing-impaired members of the church, who benefit from being able to read the manuscript after the service to pick up anything they may have missed. I then went to the sanctuary to spend time in prayer, asking God to pour out the Holy Spirit in worship, and praying that in the midst of preaching I might not get in the way of what God wanted to do—that I might disappear so that people would have the opportunity to hear from God. I pray for all those assisting in worship, from the nursery workers to the ushers. Finally, it is time for the 5:00 P.M. worship service to begin.

I am grateful for the Saturday night worship service because it actually gives me a chance to see what works and what may not work in the sermon. I think our members at Saturday night services appreciate the fact that they receive more material than the folks on Sunday morning will ever hear. I watch the facial expressions of worshipers as I preach to see if there are parts of the sermon that don't seem to connect. My wife, LaVon, worships at this service and takes notes and gives me feedback if there are places I can improve the sermon (she is very tactful in doing this—something that is very important—or we might not be married today!). That night or early Sunday morning I may actually revise my manuscript one last time based on LaVon's feedback and the response of the people at the Saturday evening service.

I know of pastors who do not prepare a manuscript. I used to preach from outlines regularly—especially when I didn't have time to prepare a manuscript. I am grateful for our hearing-impaired members, who told me it would be of help to them if they could have a manuscript. By being forced to prepare one, I must carefully think through each transition, each element in the sermon, and each detail in a way I would never do if I were preaching from an outline. The result is a better sermon. In addition, the manuscript can then be reedited for publication as a book, as was done with the 2001 Abingdon Press release *Confronting the Controversies*, which is based on a series of sermons I preached on the most controversial issues of our time.

The Value of Time Well-Spent

I will spend between fifteen and twenty hours reading, researching, preparing, praying, and writing each sermon. Could I do it in less time? Yes—earlier in my ministry I spent eight to ten hours—but I believe there was a direct correlation between the improved quality of both the content and the presentation and the increase in time spent preparing.

How can a pastor justify this amount of time spent in sermon preparation? There is nothing I do as a pastor that has a greater impact upon every part of the church's ministry, or touches more people, than the sermon. if the sermons are of a consistently high quality, people invite their friends to church, longtime church members grow in their faith and in their commitment to Christ, the offerings are stronger, and every other ministry area in the church benefits. Likewise if the sermons are weaker, every other ministry area in the church can be adversely affected.

One last word—it is critical that both you and your church set aside time for sermon preparation that is virtually nonnegotiable and during which you will not be disturbed. If you are in a small church, is there someone who can make hospital calls on the day you are doing reading, research, and preliminary writing of your sermon? Can you get away somewhere to work on your sermons where the phone won't ring and visitors won't stop by? Of course emergencies will come up—and when they do, you must take an equal amount of time from some other day during the week to compensate for lost preparation time. But the effectiveness of your preaching will be in direct proportion to the quality, undisturbed time you spend in sermon preparation. And the strength of your congregation will be in part predicated upon the effectiveness of your preaching. I have included a letter in chapter 16 written to the lay leaders of churches aimed at helping them understand how important adequate sermon preparation time is for you, and for them.

Given that preparation is essential to quality preaching, what are the other ingredients that make for effective preaching? We'll focus on this question in the next chapter.

CHAPTER FOUR

THREE CRITICAL INGREDIENTS

There are many essential ingredients to great preaching. We've mentioned several already—it must be biblical, purposeful, adequately prepared, and emerging from prayer. Throughout the rest of this book we'll mention a number of others. But it seems appropriate at this juncture to discuss three critical ingredients without which today's preachers will struggle to make their preaching effective. Sermons that affect listeners, that accomplish the purposes of preaching, are sermons that are crafted by the preacher so that they are *interesting, relevant to the hearers' lives,* and *preached with genuine passion.* Let's examine each of these in turn.

Interesting Settings and Stories

It is likely that people have never found dull preaching enticing to listen to. But in today's entertainment age, when even the national television networks feel the need to present the evening news in an entertaining way, the preacher must be able to capture and hold people's attention. The challenge is to take serious and spiritual truths, which are themselves not meant to entertain, and to place them in a context that will cause people to sit up and listen. Jesus knew how to do this. He was constantly telling stories about prodigal children, difficult neighbors, and rich people who went to hell while their poor neighbors reclined in Abraham's bosom. He used stories as a way of communicating spiritual truths, knowing he had to grab and hold the attention of his hearers in order to see true transformation.

I've known preachers who took this too far. They told story after story, but I could never discern the spiritual truths for all the stories. I've also known pastors who spent more time searching for stories than studying and preparing meaningful content. At the same time I have prepared sermons with excellent content that did not connect because I did not adequately illustrate the message.

Most of the best illustrations in my sermons don't come from a book, though I have at times searched the illustration books for help. Generally the best stories came from my own life, or from spending time listening to people and, with permission, sharing their stories. Several rules I try to apply in my own search and use of stories are: (1) I aim to never use a story about my children without asking their permission first. If they say no, I don't use the story. (2) I am cautious regarding how often I use stories about death. I knew one pastor whose congregation members, behind his back, referred to him facetiously as "Dr. Death" because every sermon ended with a story of someone dying. Yes, stories about death or the facing of death are powerful—but they are far more powerful when they are used sparingly. (3) I try to avoid using stories simply to emotionally manipulate people—some preachers seem to feel that if they can move people to tears they have succeeded in preaching an effective sermon. We all know stories that are wonderfully compelling and will move people to tears—there are times these stories are perfect illustrations of our message. But at times nearly every preacher has used these kinds of stories to make up for an otherwise ill-conceived sermon.

One of the best uses of stories can be to create an intriguing pretext for a sermon. On numerous occasions I have put myself in a position to experience something in order to be able to tell the story as a pretext, or a context, for a sermon. Allow me to give a few examples.

One evening I spent three hours in a bar, late at night, just to watch people. On Sunday I told our congregation, "This last week I spent several hours late at night in a bar. I'd like to tell you about the experience next week." People couldn't wait to hear about what their preacher had been doing in a bar late at night. I began the sermon by telling them the story of a man I watched at the bar, slowly drinking himself to a stupor, and a woman on the dance floor who danced erotically with any man who would approach her. I described a man sitting near me at the bar who told his friends, "Watch this." He then proceeded to take off his wedding ring and went out on the dance floor and danced with this woman, ultimately leaving the bar with her as they made their way to the hotel lobby adjacent to the bar to rent a room.

The events I described were all true, and they made for an interesting context into which I could begin introducing biblical stories. I told the congregation how I imagined, as I sat in that bar, Jesus walking into the room. I tried to imagine what he would say to each of these people, based upon the things Jesus said to people in the Gospels. I ended by describing Jesus speaking tenderly to the woman on the dance floor, taking her hands in his, and expressing to her how loved she is by him. I wondered at the transformation that might take place in this woman, who looked so lonely as she approached the men in the bar, if only she could know the love of Christ, and how this, not another one-night stand, was what she was looking for that night. This story naturally led to our scripture passage for the morning: Luke 7:36-50—the "sinful" woman who anointed Jesus and wept over his feet.

One evening I requested permission from the area's largest emergency room to spend two hours, from 11:00 P.M. to 1:00 A.M., just watching those who came in, and the physicians and nurses who ministered to them. What a powerful opportunity to observe life as it happens, and what powerful stories I had to share, as a pretext for preaching a sermon about the healing ministry of Jesus, how Jesus works through nurses and doctors, and the hope Jesus alone can give in the face of dark circumstances.

It is amazing what you can see if you only watch, what you hear if you only listen, and what people are willing to share with you if you only ask. Several years ago the cover story of *Newsweek* was about one of the shooting rampages that had taken place in a high school one year earlier. The story focused on healing, anger, and forgiveness. It included an interview with the husband of one of the schoolteachers who had been killed. My assistant was able to find his phone number using the Internet. I called this man, identified myself, and asked if he would mind teaching me, and through me teaching my church family, about forgiveness and moving on after such a terrible tragedy. For thirty minutes he told me his story. That Sunday I was able to share his story as we studied Jesus' teaching on forgiveness. In the end we learned that if this man, whose wife was killed by a teen with a gun, could forgive and move on, then perhaps we also could apply the teachings of Jesus in our lives.

There are a host of other examples, but these should suffice to prompt your own creativity when it comes to finding interesting stories or settings for your sermons. Again, the key is that the story not overshadow your point. After you are finished with your sermon, will they remember the point you were trying to make as they retell the story to their friends? If not, your story missed the mark.

Relevant Applications

I believe it was Harry Emerson Fosdick, writing in the first half of the last century, who said something to the effect that "people don't come to church on Sundays waiting on pins and needles to find out what happened to the Jebusites three thousand years ago." Fosdick was right. Now, that doesn't mean we shouldn't preach about the Jebusites, but we must recognize that people listen to our sermons hoping for more than a history lesson. Longtime Christians will enjoy the history lesson, but somewhere in the message there must be a personal application that they can take home with them. They want to hear, "What do the Jebusites have to do with me today?"

As you may be able to tell, I love teaching our congregation the Bible—I love to study, and I love to pass on to them the knowledge I have gained. But what I have learned is that most will tune me out if they feel that the information I share with them has no connection to their lives. However, if they know that somewhere during the sermon I am going to bring the message back to their lives and the present day, they usually will enjoy learning new biblical information. So when we studied Moses for eight weeks a couple of years ago, I was able to pique their interest up front because Moses is such a towering figure in the Bible—yes, they were interested in knowing more about him. But this interest would have lasted about two sermons had I not, from the beginning, helped them understand how Moses' story is preserved in sacred scripture in large part because his story is also our story. I spent ten minutes at the beginning of the first sermon teaching them about the Hyksos invasion of Egypt seventeen hundred years before Christ, and the subsequent expulsion of the Hyksos, and the relationship between these two events and the oppression of the Hebrews in the time Moses was born. They were willing to hear the history lesson, which was an important one for understanding the Exodus, because they knew that at some point the historical information would offer a key to unlocking something important for their lives. They knew that soon I would talk about the connection between the fearful pharaoh and the fears that lurk in our hearts; as I told them about Shiphrah and Puah, the Hebrew midwives who refused to obey Pharaoh and put to death the Hebrew children, they knew that somewhere would follow a lesson on courage along with a concrete challenge for us to live as they lived; and when I told them of the compassionate princess who saved Moses—a most unlikely choice of heroines—they knew that somehow this would tie back in to God's providence and the mysterious ways God works in our lives.

We've all learned that the critical question we must ask before we are finished writing our sermons is simply this: "So what?" If you cannot clearly offer an answer to that question at the end of your sermon, it is not yet finished.

Passionate Presentations

Several months ago I attended a special concert—part of a classical music series that our church was hosting in partnership with the Friends of Chamber Music. While I occasionally listen to classical music, I was raised on rock and roll. I attended this event just to show my support. The program featured a guest artist on piano—an incredibly gifted person trained in the classical tradition. But the real power of the evening came from the emcee of the event who spent the evening teaching us about the classical music of various artists—and his excitement, enthusiasm, and passion were contagious. I had a wonderful evening and came away with a great appreciation for the various forms of music he taught about. This is the power of passion!

On the opposite end of the spectrum, I recently ate supper in a new restaurant. When the waitress came to take our order I asked what she liked best on the menu. She casually shrugged her shoulders and said, "I have never eaten here myself, but I hear others say they like the steak." I have heard preachers who preached like this. They spoke of great spiritual truths as though they were themselves not convinced of their veracity, and had perhaps not experienced the things they were preaching about firsthand.

I recently read a book on executive leadership in the corporate world that noted one of the most important indicators of whether a business leader will be successful is the degree of passion they exhibit for their "product or service." Nowhere is this more true than in the pulpit. When you are convinced that the word you are preaching is true, that it is an authentic word from the Lord, and when you have actually sought to live this word, or have seen it work in your life—and when you can get excited about this important word you have to share, others will sit up and take notice.

I once spoke at a conference for laity and clergy where two laypeople took me aside after lunch and said, "Can you please help us? Our pastor is a good man; he has many gifts. But his personality is so lethargic; he simply doesn't get excited about anything. It really hurts us in worship because his lethargy sets the tone for everything else. We just wish there was some way for him to express a little enthusiasm once in a while." I know this was in large part the man's personality—my only suggestion, a bit tongue in cheek, was that they ask him to drink several cups of espresso before worship each week! It is hard to conjure up passion—but it is not impossible. When you understand the importance of this, you approach the preaching moment as though it is a battle and your passion is the key to victory. There have been Sundays over my twelve years at Church of the Resurrection when I was physically ill, or simply tired—my natural supply of passion was exhausted. But at those times I mustered up what strength I had to present the message with passion and conviction.

Sermon Structure

One final word about the shape of our sermons. Preaching professors sometimes speak of two basic types of sermons. The first type begins with the human condition or the problem facing human beings and then draws the hearers toward the teaching of scripture and God's solution to the problem. This first type of sermon starts where we itch, and then brings the scripture to bear offering God's solution, challenge, or timely word. The second type begins with the scriptures, usually with a scriptural truth, and then seeks to apply that truth to our daily lives.

I use both models in preaching. Generally nonreligious and nominally religious people are more readily drawn to the former. Many of the people who attend the Church of the Resurrection are not yet sure if they are believers, and they certainly are not convinced that the Bible is God's inspired Word. So announcing that we will study the eighth chapter of Romans for eight weeks doesn't excite them. But announcing a series of sermons on God's work through tragedy, on overcoming challenges, and finding strength to persevere—all of which are addressed in Romans chapter 8—will see the unchurched arriving in anticipation of finding answers to the questions and struggles they face.

This issue points to the importance of sermon structure. How you organize your sermons is almost as important as creating excellent content. This is one of the benefits of working on sermons over a period of days—you have the time to reflect on the structure to see if it works. People are often surprised that I seem to preach without notes. I am able to do this when the sermon structure makes sense and there is a logical progression that naturally leads to an important or climactic conclusion.

CHAPTER FIVE

USING VIDEO IN PREACHING AND WORSHIP

M any of you reading this chapter are already using video in worship and to provide support for your sermons. To you I will offer several words of advice and encouragement, along with a few ideas. More than half of you reading this chapter likely have yet to introduce video into worship. I want to begin by offering a few words of encouragement to you.

There can be no doubt that the use of multimedia in worship and in preaching is here to stay. It can be a powerful tool to enhance the worship experience and to aid in the communication process in your preaching. Choosing not to introduce this medium into worship at this time is not unlike a story I heard Lyle Schaller recently tell of a church that refused to introduce indoor bathrooms when sewers became available in their town, preferring to maintain their outhouses because they felt it sacrilegious to have toilets in the house of the Lord!

It is not essential to have indoor toilets in a church, especially if the congregation's only concern is ministry to those who are already in the church, who are used to outhouses. For about ten to fifteen years that little church continued to do just fine with its outhouses. But eventually, inviting people to use outhouses seemed so anachronistic that it became a statement about the church: It did not wish to connect with contemporary people. This was a barrier to reaching out to a new generation of people. I believe the same will be true of the use of video in worship.

Introducing Video into Worship

From 1990 to 1998 we only occasionally used video in worship—rolling in a series of big-screen televisions to show an occasional stewardship video. We grew rapidly during that period of time, and we did this without video. I clearly believe that churches can still, at this time, successfully reach people without video in worship. But I also know that our worship, and especially my preaching, has been greatly enhanced as a result of the addition of video. There are entire series of sermons that I could never have done were it not for this tool.

Most churches can accommodate video—in smaller churches this could be accomplished with one or two big-screen televisions set high enough that all can see them, and with a bright enough picture to compensate for ambient light. Beyond this, simple wiring, a VCR, a simple switcher, and a computer could be all you need for providing a level of video support for your worship and sermons. This could be accomplished for under $10,000. If you built your system with used equipment, and members were willing to donate a computer, VCR, and big-screen televisions, you might be able to build a system for the cost of a switcher and cabling.

(For more information on the technical side of introducing video in worship I would encourage you and those staff interested in introducing video in worship to attend the Church of the Resurrection Leadership Institute where we offer workshops and the opportunity to learn tips and clues from our staff on how to effectively use video in worship. You can find out more about this annual event by contacting the church at www.cor.org.)

Most churches will go beyond this simple video arrangement I've described. At Church of the Resurrection, we have the equivalent of a small television studio that supports our video ministry, and we have made a significant investment of staff and resources because we believe in its importance to the future of our ministry.

The challenge for most churches will not be the raising of funds to be able to purchase the equipment for introducing video into worship. Your challenges will be in helping your members accept this new medium (some will complain) and in overcoming the temptation to go overboard with this new tool (a frequent problem with video in worship). Let's talk about these two challenges for a moment.

Acceptance

The Church of the Resurrection was only eight years old when we introduced video in worship. Most of our members were under the age of fifty. And yet the moment we started using video screens, we got complaints. There were not a lot of complaints— maybe a dozen that first six months—but they were very loud. Two families left the church (although one eventually came back). They complained that we had capitulated to the culture, that they did not want to come to church to "watch television"— they could do this at home. They wrote how it cheapened worship. And because we were a bit nervous about this ourselves, each letter was painful. But we continued to explain to our congregation why this tool was important in reaching a new generation of people, and how it would enhance the worship experience. We described this as a time in history similar to when electricity was introduced into churches and light and sound systems were added to sanctuaries. We acknowledged the feelings of those who were not supportive, and we asked for the congregation's support as we took these steps forward. We tried to demonstrate the power of this new tool—but we did so gently and conservatively.

The result was that six months after introducing video we had a holiday weekend when we gave our video team the weekend off—and church members complained because we didn't have video! Today no one in our church questions the importance of this tool for ministry. My point is, be prepared for this. In fact, you may even want to tell your congregation our church's story before you use video for the first time in your church.

One of the videos we have produced, which I felt was very compelling, endearing, and demonstrated the power of video to the older generation in our church, was used during the offertory one Sunday (it was three minutes in length—too long for use in the sermon). I was preaching a series of sermons on marriage, and we decided to interview couples in our church who had been married for more than fifty years. We asked them to teach the younger people in our congregation what it takes to stay married for more than half a century. The video was wonderfully edited, and it featured six couples sharing humorous stories and offering touching advice on marriage. If there were any of our seniors who did not see the value of video prior to that weekend, their opposition faded as they saw their friends on the video screen and watched the effect that video had on the entire congregation.

I mentioned two concerns—the second was the temptation to overuse video in worship, and here is where I will transition to speak not only to those of you who have yet to introduce video in worship, but also to those of you who already have video in your sanctuary.

Control

In the mid-1980s, when Apple Computer introduced the first Postscript laser printers to the mass market—printers that allowed you to print in hundreds of fonts (something virtually unknown at the time)—suddenly desktop publishing became accessible to the masses. I remember those days; everyone began developing their own newsletters—with forty different fonts per page! We were so enamored with the power of our computers and printers, we didn't know when to stop. And the graphic artists out there just cringed. We novices didn't know about the importance of white space in a document, or the rule that a document should generally stick to using two or at the most three fonts. We didn't realize there was a reason, when newspaper publishers had access to hundreds of fonts, they settled on a handful of more conservative typestyles.

The same is true now that video is in the hands of the masses. I have attended churches where the video seemed to be the focus of the worship service. I have heard sermons that seemed to be written entirely because the pastor wanted to use a certain video clip in church. When it comes to video, like fonts in a newsletter, sometimes "less is more."

At Church of the Resurrection our video screens are not located at the center of the chancel, but off to the sides. The locations of the screens themselves is meant to say that this is not the focal point of worship. Because of the size of our sanctuary we use what is known as "IMAG"—image magnification—which means that what is happening in worship is appearing simultaneously on the screen. This allows our congregation members sitting in the rear of the sanctuary to see the faces of those we baptize, to see my facial expressions as I preach, and to be closer to the "action" through the video screens. This in itself is a powerful help in communicating and preaching when you have a larger sanctuary.

Before worship begins we have a series of slides that appear on the screens publicizing upcoming events in the life of our church. Just before worship begins we may show a short video promo for one of the events (Tip: Don't use more than one video promo a week. It will diminish the power of each if you use more than one). Immediately prior to the worship service start a slide comes up that says, "Welcome to the Church of the Resurrection."

We design graphic backgrounds for each sermon series. Often we'll use classical art of biblical scenes that we're focusing on in a particular sermon as a way of integrating art and worship. We have three cameras shooting the worship service, and one member of our staff is in the control room changing which shot appears on the screens—this makes the image magnification more pleasant to watch for those sitting in the back of the room. If you are planning on using IMAG, a minimum of two cameras is important, and the ideal is three or more.

The image of the worship leaders appears on the screen most of the time, but when we begin to sing, the words to the hymns or songs appear on the screen. We have hymnals in our seats, but there are very few people who use them today—most people seem to prefer to look up and sing, rather than looking down at the hymnal. This has improved the quality of congregational singing as well. (Tip: As you are projecting your lyrics, always move to the next verse or set of lyrics before the congregation is done singing the words on the current screen—the eye is always scanning just ahead of where we are singing, which means worshipers have the last three or four words in their minds before they sing, but they cannot be ready to sing the next line if it is not on the screen before it is needed.)

So far, what I have described of Church of the Resurrection use of video is fairly simple. Our members can ignore the video screens altogether if they choose. The screens have been an enhancement, but not a focal point.

This same philosophy carries through to the sermon. My personal preference as a preacher is to have people making eye contact with me, not the video screens. Which means that while our people have sermon outlines in their bulletins, we do not use PowerPoint style presentations during the sermons. I have actually found that in many venues, not simply sermons, PowerPoint style presentations detract from the speaker rather than enhancing what they are saying. I have attended presentations where the philosophy of some seemed to be, "I have all this capability on my laptop and my video projector—I need to use it." The most effective speakers applied the principle: "Just because I can do this doesn't mean I should" or, again, "Less is more."

So, in our sermons we don't highlight certain points by placing them on the video screens. If I am using multiple scripture references, we will put the text of the scriptures on the screens so people can read along with me—this helps reinforce the power of the scripture and helps those persons who did not bring their Bibles to church or who do not know their Bibles well enough to quickly locate a certain book of the Bible.

Let's take a look at the other uses of video we have made during various sermons.

Other Uses of Video

As I have already mentioned, during our study of the letters of Paul in 2002, each week the sermon would begin with a bit of historical background related to the specific letter we were focusing on. I would call for a map of the particular missionary journey on which Paul founded the church. We would then zoom in for a closer look at the location of the city. Shortly after this I would call for a thirty-second video compiled from footage I shot while visiting the ruins of the cities to which Paul sent his letters. Among the most powerful of these videos was that of Philippi; you can still see what tradition holds is the prison cell where Paul and Silas were placed after having been stripped naked and beaten. The opportunity to actually show this place was a powerful addition—it made the story real and concrete. In many of the sermons on Paul, this was the only use of video and graphic images—all at the beginning of the sermon, but this was a powerful addition and helped our worshipers actually understand the story.

A more intensive use of video was in our series of sermons on love, marriage, and sex. In preparation for this series of sermons I spent twenty hours interviewing various couples in our church about the state of their marriages. Based on these interviews, I asked our video team to reinterview these couples, asking them specific questions based on my earlier interviews. These interviews were used in each of the nine sermons on this topic. I often used two interviews at different points in the sermon. The power of this use of video was that these couples were real people in the congregation, telling their actual stories, which either illustrated the point I had just made or led to the point I was about to make. Some of them were very humorous. Some were much more serious. But all were very powerful. Five years earlier I had preached a similar series, only that time we did not have video and I only quoted from my interviews with couples. This time, with the ability to use video, the resulting sermons were much more powerful.

Among the more intriguing uses of video for us was a series of sermons we did in 2001 entitled, "The Gospel and the Stories Making News Today." In this series we partnered with the local ABC affiliate in Kansas City (see the DVD that came with this book for the promo for that series, which we showed on Easter to announce the upcoming sermons). Each week the sermon would start with one of the local anchors reporting from the news desk on a story that had aired that week. They would end their story by saying, "And now we turn to you, Reverend Hamilton, as we look to hear the connection between the gospel and this story making news today." In most of these sermons, this was the only video used, but it was the basic jumping-off point for the entire sermon, which then looked at the theological and ethical dimension to the story and a possible Christian response (I'll describe the content of this series in more detail in chapter 10).

There are a host of other ways we have made use of video in sermons, some of which you will learn about in subsequent chapters. These are meant to open your creativity in thinking through how you would make use of this powerful medium. Before closing this chapter, allow me to offer a few tips and hints that may be helpful.

- If you are going to use clips of commercial films you should purchase the Motion Picture Licensing Corporation (MPLC) License, available by calling 1-800-462-8855 or going to their Web site at www.mplc.com.
- When using film clips, we avoid using R-rated films. This is a matter of principle for us, even though it means not using some powerful film scenes. We want to discourage support for films that include gratuitous sex or violence, and

encourage the production of more films that are PG in rating. The use of video clips from a film is giving the church's tacit support for that film.

- When it comes to using film clips, we do this rarely—perhaps four to six times per year. Be cautious about using a powerful film clip to salvage an otherwise subpar sermon; develop a great sermon and allow the film clip to help drive the point home.
- Video clips in the midst of a sermon should, as a rule, be no longer than one and a half to two minutes. Most video clips we use are under one minute. That means more time must be spent editing down a video interview—but here again, less is more. If you consider a thirty-minute sermon as standard, and a video is three minutes in length, 10 percent of the sermon was devoted to that one clip. There are exceptions, but as a general rule, this is too much time to devote to one clip.
- Be very careful in choosing what images you place on the screen. We have children in every worship service, and we have to be careful that the images we use are not too strong, or frightening, or otherwise inappropriate for kids.
- Sometimes a story told is far more powerful than a story watched. Seldom is watching a movie based on a book as enjoyable as reading the book. This is because as we read the book we can use our own imagination to see the characters and the unfolding of events. The same is true with illustrations: Often, telling someone else's story is more powerful than interviewing the person telling their own story.
- Video is a great way to allow for testimonials. We prefer to tape testimonials, which allows us to control the length and to edit out elements that would be less helpful. If you are using testimonials for stewardship campaigns, video is the way to go in most cases.
- The use of music under video can be very important. Take a feature-length film and remove the musical score, and it is amazing how much less powerful the video is. Some video

clips you produce for worship do not need a sound track, but many will benefit from the music's impact.

- Don't forget your choir as you are planning to add video capabilities in your sanctuary—they will need to see and hear the video as well!

Among the ideas that are beginning to gain acceptance is that of entire sermons being offered on video. There are several churches across the United States that currently simulcast their worship services, or at least their sermons, to multiple locations where worshipers actually watch the sermon on video. Several churches who were between pastors have purchased our sermons on video and used them on Sunday mornings. These were small churches who had their own lay worship leaders and choir programs. For the price of the videotape, they were able to offer a series of sermons of their choosing with high-quality graphics and video components. Lyle Schaller and others have suggested that this may very well be the wave of the future for many smaller churches who will be able to choose from a variety of the most effective preachers of the day, and their choice of sermon series or studies, to present in their pulpit each week through video.

Another use of video we have found effective at the Church of the Resurrection is Web streaming. We post each week's sermon on our Web site by Wednesday or Thursday of the following week. We have had notes and calls from people around the world who have viewed these sermons at any hour of the day or night. If you preached a sermon that one of your members felt was particularly pertinent to a friend, a friend who did not go to church or could not attend church, with an e-mail featuring a Web link they could invite their friend to watch the sermon in the convenience of their own home at any time.

Finally, we have been grateful for the opportunity to use closed-circuit video as a way of making room for additional persons in worship when our sanctuary has been full. On this last Christmas Eve we had just over thirteen thousand in attendance for our seven candlelight services. But our sanctuary would accommodate only eleven thousand during those seven services.

Two thousand persons worshiped via video in our narthex and a second video overflow room. We positioned song leaders in each room, along with ushers and greeters, and pastors in robes spent time connecting with each person in that room. Without video capabilities we would have turned away a significant number of people who would never have come back. Prior to construction of our current sanctuary, we used closed-circuit video in an overflow room every weekend for four months, asking our most committed members to worship in the overflow room (we bribed them with lemonade, gourmet coffee, cookies, and a leatherbound study Bible for their household!). More than four hundred accepted the challenge and made room for our visitors.

The use of video in worship is just one of the reasons it is important to have a team of volunteers or staff who will work together to design the highest-quality worship experience possible. Let's turn our attention to the Worship Planning Team.

CHAPTER SIX

The Worship Planning Team

I have made reference several times to our worship planning team. This seems an appropriate juncture at which to describe their work. Bear in mind, the team that for us is composed of paid staff may for you be a volunteer team that meets one evening a week after everyone is off work to do the same kind of work our staff do on Monday mornings. The take-away from this chapter will not be the exact composition or size of your worship planning team, but instead the idea of working together with a group of people who can help enhance the total quality of the worship experience.

With this in mind, let's join a typical worship planning meeting in progress:

It's 10:00 A.M. on Monday, and sitting around the table are the following persons, beginning on my left:

The minister of Music and Celebration Arts, who oversees the total music ministry of the church.

The executive director of Worship and Caring Ministries, who is a senior staff member and a pastor. This person coordinates and is the direct supervisor of most of the team in the room.

The pastors of Caring Ministries—we have three of these pastors, who all are present for part of this meeting. Each week, they write and offer the pastoral prayer, which is shaped by what they learn about the focus of the weekend's worship services at this meeting.

The executive assistant to the senior pastor—my assistant, who takes notes for the meetings, offers input, and does sermon research for me based on the information gleaned from these meetings.

The director of Saving Grace Productions, who heads our video ministries.

The assistant director of Saving Grace Productions, who focuses on producing materials needed to support the sermon.

The director of Contemporary Worship, who is the musical leader of our contemporary services and selects the music for these services based on the sermon themes.

The administrative assistant to executive staff, who takes notes and coordinates details on behalf of our executive directors.

The director of Worship Ministries, who is responsible for the appearance of the sanctuary, banners, and visuals, and oversees the ushers and communion ministries. This person handles most of the logistical details related to worship.

We begin by sharing joys and concerns, and then we open with prayer, inviting the Holy Spirit to guide our meeting and lead us in worship preparation. We then spend fifteen minutes talking about what went well and what needed improvement in the previous weekend's worship services. Our aim is constant improvement. Every week there is some aspect of worship that we are tweaking and adjusting. We then talk about upcoming worship services—beginning with those things a bit farther out. This week we will continue our discussion on the schedule for Candlelight Christmas Eve so that all other affected departments can have this information (our aim is to make these decisions four months out). We look at upcoming sermons in our series and any special needs we may have several weeks out. We talk about any special announcements or videos to be used in worship in the upcoming weekend.

Finally we begin discussion of the upcoming sermon. I walk through the basic outline of the sermon and the main point as I understand it at this juncture (based upon the sermon plan developed months earlier). I invite our staff to give their input or ideas. How might we illustrate this point? What is your experience with this issue? This discussion is sometimes very fruitful and adds a great deal to my thinking as I begin working on the sermon in earnest. Sometimes the team has little to add to the discussion, and that is okay too.

A chart is handed out for each of the weekend's six worship services, showing the special music and the choice of hymns or praise songs, as well as any other special events taking place in worship. This chart is put together by the music department but includes information gleaned from earlier worship team meetings regarding video, scriptures, baptisms, and other elements in the weekend's worship services. The songs were chosen based on the sermon outlines handed out to the worship planning team several months earlier. At this meeting we occasionally change a hymn or suggest a different song based on the day's discussion of the sermon themes.

We break by 11:30 or 12:00 for each of the team members to begin working with their staff and volunteers to prepare for the weekend's worship service. Throughout the week I will likely be in contact with the video department a few more times. I may e-mail photos or scriptures to them for inclusion in the sermon. We may talk back and forth about video ideas. If they are producing a video or editing a film clip for me to consider using for the sermon they will get that to me by Thursday for a final approval. Many times I am still getting information to them on Friday to be added to the sermon. This is not ideal, but it is reality. They function much better with a bit more time to work on inputting information or graphics into our computer system—but they are an amazing team who do whatever it takes to make things work. Most of those who input our scriptures and songs are volunteers who do an amazing job, giving countless hours to supporting this ministry.

During the weekend's worship services we are still tweaking things. We may find that a video we had planned for the beginning of the sermon actually works better at the end, or perhaps doesn't work at all. We may see that we need to drop one verse from a particular hymn, or add another. We try to minimize these kinds of changes, but they do happen nearly every weekend, and the teams and volunteers are flexible and willing to adapt.

How does this idea of a worship planning team translate into a small church where you may have no other staff? As I mentioned at the beginning of this chapter, it is entirely possible that you may have a team of laity who would be truly honored to be part of the worship team. One may focus on working with a banner and altar guild, another works with the choir or praise band, another— probably a young person—loves to work with computer video editing and has a team of volunteers who help with this. You may have one member of your team who is a film buff, and he or she has a team of friends who will bounce around ideas of scenes from films that might support your upcoming sermons. You may even have a librarian or someone who just loves searching the Internet who will volunteer to do research for upcoming sermons for you. This team could be a powerhouse for you and for the church—and not one of them paid staff. As your church grows, these may be the persons you end up hiring for these positions.

One last word about the planning team—what I have described is how we were doing things at the end of 2002. My guess is that this will change in the future as even the worship planning team seeks to improve our planning processes.

CHAPTER SEVEN

FISHING EXPEDITION SERMONS

I n chapter 1, I wrote of the five aims of my preaching: Evangelism, Discipleship, Pastoral Care, Equipping and Sending, and Institutional Development. There are individual sermons that accomplish two or even three of these aims. Within a given series of sermons I may have sermons that accomplish each of these aims. But in my planning for a year's worth of sermons, certain whole series will lean more toward one or the other of these aims. Specific series are planned, from their inception, to reach large numbers of unchurched people, giving our members an opportunity to encourage their friends to attend. Other series are clearly aimed at deepening the faith of those who are already Christians. My hope is that during the evangelistic sermons I am still offering something that ministers to and deepens the faith of our most committed Christians. I am also hopeful that the sermons aimed at deepening our members' faith have elements that are attractive to the unchurched. Yet these are distinct emphases for different sermon series.

In the next five chapters I will look at each of these aims and offer concrete examples of these types of sermons that I hope will encourage your own thinking on how to approach these same aims in your preaching. Let's begin with a discussion of evangelistic sermon series and evangelistic preaching.

Evangelism

In large part the growth of the Church of the Resurrection has been driven by Candlelight Christmas Eve and the sermon series that we have announced following this holiday. The candlelight Christmas Eve service is one of the most powerful and emotive services of the year, and the unchurched will come to these services if invited. Even longtime unchurched persons are looking for the deeper meaning of Christmas by Christmas Eve. If they have children they likely want their children to experience a candlelight service, because most adults in America have experienced a candlelight service at some time in their childhood, even if today they do not attend church. We have sent direct mailings to the community inviting them to our Candlelight Christmas Eve, and we provide our members with beautiful color postcards or brochures to use as invitations to their friends.

On Christmas Eve we generally double our worship attendance from its fall average. We hold our first candlelight services on the twenty-third and ask our most committed members to come the night before Christmas Eve to make room for visitors on the December 24. In 2002, the Monday evening service on December 23 was the second most crowded of the candlelight services—it was a packed house! Many who enjoy this service are heading out of town for the holiday. On the twenty-fourth we have six services beginning at 3:00 P.M. (we darken the windows of the sanctuary for the candlelight portion of the service). We advertise the 3:00 and 5:00 P.M. services for those with small children, and these are usually full.

Our aim throughout these services is to offer the highest-quality worship service possible, with great music and a twenty-five-minute sermon that is clearly designed to speak to the unchurched about the need for and meaning of Christmas. At the beginning and end of this service we will take a moment to announce our upcoming sermon series, which will begin the second week of January (we've found that folks are not back in town from the Christmas break the first week of January). We usually show a short video promo for the January sermon series (see the DVD that came with your book to view the opening announcement at our Christmas Eve service in 2002 with the video promo for our January 2003 sermon series entitled, "Christianity and the Religions of the World"). We will also have a postcard that advertises the upcoming sermons (samples of these cards are also featured on the DVD). If the series of sermons is enticing to the unchurched, we will see a significant increase in worship attendance in January over our prior year's attendance.

We call these January sermon series "fishing expeditions," drawing from Jesus' invitation to the first disciples to become "fishers of people." Our aim is to cast out the net on Christmas Eve when the largest number of nonreligious and nominally religious people are present in our worship, and try to encourage them to return for worship after the holidays. I'll share with you four of the fishing expedition series of sermons I have preached in recent years.

Most Frequently Asked Questions

At Christmas Eve services in 1996, we handed out a questionnaire to all present inviting them to write down the questions they really wished a pastor or church would deal with—questions that kept them or their friends or loved ones from faith. There were fourteen hundred questions submitted that night. We announced that beginning the second week of January we would tackle the eight most frequently asked questions, allowing those present to actually set the agenda for that sermon series. In

January worship attendance increased by 40 percent over the average attendance of the prior month!

We could have guessed the questions people would ask. But by inviting them to fill out the survey, we allowed them to have input and make this sermon series their own. Here are a few of the topics or questions we addressed in this sermon series:

Why do bad things happen to good people?
Why do my prayers go unanswered?
How do we reconcile the miracles of the Bible with modern science?
Is Christianity the only way?
What about hypocritical Christians, ungodly preachers, and organized religion?

In this sermon series each message was an opportunity to do a bit of Christian apologetics, and hence a chance to help longtime Christians "give an account of their faith." Our members struggled with how to answer the faith questions of their unchurched friends and family. In addition, these questions plague the hearts of many churched people as well as the unchurched. But for the unchurched this was a chance to hear a pastor take seriously their questions.

In the last sermon in this series I said to our congregation, "For the last few weeks I have taken the hardest questions you had to ask about faith. I offered answers to these questions. Now it is time for me to ask you a question. And just as I didn't dodge your questions, I don't want you to dodge this one—it is a question Jesus himself asked those who came to hear him: "Who do you say that I am?" This is the question I want you to wrestle with today—who do you say Jesus is? Having dealt with your questions, I want to invite you today to take the next step, and to choose to become one of his followers." I ended the sermon in this way, and then led the congregation in a prayer in which those present could commit their lives to Christ. The result was that hundreds of people became followers of Christ—but this outcome began with a plan to reach those persons who would visit our church on Christmas Eve.

Controversial Issues

Let's take a look at another fishing expedition series of sermons. On Christmas Eve of 1999 we announced to worshipers that beginning the second week of January we would launch a series of sermons on the most difficult and controversial issues of our time. A postcard in the bulletin outlined what those topics would be. We invited worshipers to join us for a bit of controversy as we wrestled with hard issues. The second Sunday of January our worship attendance increased by one thousand people over what it had been running in the last quarter of 1999!

These sermons were an opportunity not only for evangelism, but also pastoral care. Our longtime church members were presented the opportunity to do social ethics—to apply their faith to complex moral issues. We probably lost a handful of members during this series—but we kept most of those one thousand new people who began attending. I received hundreds of e-mails during the sermon series. People were talking about these sermons at work, sharing them with their congresspersons—the response was amazing.

Here are the issues we dealt with:

The Separation of Church and State
Evolution in the Public Schools
The Death Penalty
Euthanasia
Prayer in Public Schools
Abortion
Homosexuality

We saved the most controversial issues for the end as a climax. We set a new record for worship attendance on the day we preached on homosexuality—we had twenty-five hundred more in worship than we had averaged just two months earlier. (This series of sermons was published by Abingdon Press as *Confronting the Controversies* and includes study questions for group use. The video- and audiotapes are available from the Church of the Resurrection at www.cor.org.)

The basic premise of this series of sermons was that all these issues are moral issues, and moral issues are meant to be shaped by values, and values are shaped by faith. As such, these are important issues to discuss in church. In addition to drawing in a large number of unchurched people who were amazed that a church was willing to deal with these topics, we offered pastoral care (especially in the sermons on euthanasia, abortion, and homosexuality) and, as noted above, taught Christian social ethics and how to apply the scriptures to complex issues, thus accomplishing the aim of discipleship as well.

I will say that this series of sermons required more research, reading, and study than any other series I have ever done. I spent an average of twenty hours on each message and have research files that are two and three inches thick. My assistant, Sue Thompson, was invaluable in helping me prepare for these messages, as was our video ministry, who were able to pull together pertinent video materials from various sources. I will describe in more detail how we approached these sermons, and others like them, in chapter 12 when we discuss preaching on difficult topics.

I'll offer two more fishing expedition series to rouse your own creativity:

The Problem of Evil

When asked to describe their primary reason for not pursuing faith, unchurched people will nearly always refer to the problem of evil. Every night on the evening news there is story after story that seems to them to be an affront to belief in a good and loving God. On Christmas Eve of 2000 we asked these questions to our worshipers: "Have you ever wondered how a good and loving

God could allow suffering? Have you ever been profoundly disappointed with God? Have you ever prayed and prayed for God to heal someone and nothing happened? If so, we encourage you to join us for a series of sermons we'll be offering beginning the second week of January entitled, 'Where Was God When . . .' "

This series was shorter than most—I felt the topic was so heavy I did not want to carry it beyond three weeks. The subtitle of the series was, "The Problem of Evil and the Providence of God." In this series of sermons I wanted not only to reach the unchurched, but to help our church members develop an adequate doctrine of providence. This series of sermons accomplished evangelism, discipleship, and pastoral care aims in each message. The result was once again staggering. Worship attendance rose from five thousand in December of 2000 to over six thousand per weekend in January of 2001.

Each week the sermon began with a video interview of people in our congregation who had faced tragic circumstances, and then the sermon unpacked the tragedy and the theological questions it raised. The interviews were compelling—you could hear a pin drop in the congregation at the end of each story—and it was obvious those present were wondering, *How do we reconcile faith in a loving God with this story?* The challenge in this series was to "de-construct" most worshipers' views about providence. Most Christians, even committed believers, have a doctrine of how God works in the world that they learned when they were small children—which indicates that if they are good people and they serve God, nothing bad will happen to them. When something bad happens to them, or someone they love, they are left confused and distraught because God did not do what they expected. They are left wondering if the tragedy was punishment from God, or a sign that there is no God, or God's attempt to teach them a lesson. In each of the first two sermons I took apart this view of providence. Finally, in the third sermon, I came back to focus entirely on rebuilding an adequate doctrine of providence—of how God is at work in our world.

I cannot begin to convey the number of people who came to me after that to tell me their stories—how they had been away from the church for years and years because they were angry or disappointed with God, and now, for the first time, they understood how God works in the world, and they were reclaiming their faith.

Love, Marriage, and Sex

Finally, allow me to share with you the fishing expedition that brought in so many fish we couldn't accommodate them all. On Christmas Eve of 2001 we announced that we would be launching a series of sermons entitled, "Biblical Perspectives on Love, Marriage, and Sex." We had surveyed our congregation five weeks earlier so that we could have time to adequately prepare these sermons and the marketing for them. We announced that these sermons were based on the actual results of the largest survey of married and single people ever conducted in our area (2,400-plus surveys were returned) and that each week we would be honestly dealing with the kind of relationship issues people in this community were wrestling with, turning to the Bible for wisdom and insights that could help real people have the kind of relationships God intended.

Several months of preparation went into this series of sermons. I mentioned briefly in chapter 5 that I had begun interviewing couples in November, just to spend time with other married persons talking about the issues they faced in marriage. We ran a bulletin announcement inviting any couples who would be willing to sit down and talk with me about their marriages to call. We had sixteen couples who volunteered, and every Thursday afternoon for a month I visited with them, one couple at a time, interviewing them and looking for information that could be helpful in designing this sermon series.

In December we administered the survey you will find on the enclosed DVD (you are welcome to reproduce the survey for your use, though it is likely you will want to design your own survey). We handed this out one Sunday morning in worship, and I explained to the congregation that I was preparing for a series of sermons designed to help couples and singles, even children and teens, in understanding God's plan for the relationship between a man and a woman. I told them I needed their input and asked if they would take five minutes during the service to fill out a simple questionnaire. If they preferred they could take it home and return it. We stopped the service, provided background music, and gave them time to fill these out. Then we asked if they were not finished with the survey to take time during the offertory—another three minutes—to complete it. Afterward, my assistant gathered a small team of people to collate the information and summarize it in a way that would help me prepare for these sermons.

In addition to this background, we went back and video-interviewed some of those couples I had met with in person in November, and then interviewed couples we knew in our church who had been married more than fifty years. I also met with a Christian psychologist and a marriage and family counselor to hear their perspectives on these issues. Finally, I purchased about a dozen books that were recommended by the therapists and others as the best resources on marriage today. All this research and preparation formed the backdrop for this series of sermons.

The resulting increase in number of worshipers was staggering. Our sanctuary at that time seated only 1,600 people. We had six worship services and had been averaging in December just under 6,000 per weekend in worship. The first Sunday of this series we had 7,500 people show up. This was what we anticipated as a possibility, and it stretched our facilities thin. On that Sunday we announced that the following weekend I would share with them information from the surveys on "what women wish men knew about women" (this sermon is found on the enclosed DVD). That following Sunday 9,200 people showed up! We had nowhere to put them—we used every metal folding chair in the building. We set worshipers in front of television screens in the narthex. They sat on the floors and up the stairs leading to the balcony. We even invited some to sit with the choir in the choir loft.

Despite a meltdown in every part of our ministry that weekend, they all showed up the next weekend when we spoke about "what men wish women knew about men." Unfortunately, despite very positive reviews of the messages and worship, we could not keep these folks. It took twenty minutes to get out of the parking lot after each service. We ran out of room in the nurseries and Sunday school. We did keep many of these newcomers—about one thousand joined the church; but we lost two thousand we might have kept had we had the capacity for them (as of the printing of this book the church is building a larger sanctuary, which will double our worship capacity as well as nurseries, Sunday school, and parking).

One last word on this series of sermons. As is the case with most series, we were not only doing evangelism, we were offering pastoral care (a number of couples reported that this series of sermons was pivotal in saving their marriages or helping them through difficult places in their marriage), and we were teaching people the implications of being a Christian, and the significance of the Scriptures, to the relationship between a man and a woman. At the end of the sermon series I gave this invitation: "We've been talking for nine weeks about what relationships can look like and what they were meant to be—but it is impossible to experience what I have been describing to you apart from a relationship with Jesus Christ and a shared common faith that forms the foundation for authentic Christian marriages. So today, I would like to give you the opportunity to actually take that next step in moving toward the kind of marriage we have been studying, by giving you the opportunity to pray, and talk to God, and commit your life to Christ." Once again there were hundreds who made this commitment.

What is the take-away from this chapter for you? If you do a good job of inviting people to Christmas Eve services, if your worship on that night is excellent, and if you announce on that evening a series of compelling sermons that are designed to meet the real needs of nominally and nonreligious people, they will return. And these sermon series will not only minister to the unchurched, but they will bless and minister to your churched folks as well.

A Postscript on Altar Calls

I would like to offer a final word of challenge to preachers on both sides of the theological spectrum regarding the "altar call." Some of you reading this book come from a tradition that feels a sermon is not a sermon without an altar call. I do not want to diminish this in any way, but I do want to say that the unchurched sometimes perceive this as every sermon being the same salvation message with a different scripture text and different illustrations. Some unchurched are turned off by what they perceive to be a kind of manipulation in the invitation itself. It may be worth rethinking the concept of the altar call and asking the question: "How and when in a sermon series would an altar call be most effective?"

I recently went shopping for a car. I just wanted to kick a few tires—I wasn't really ready to buy yet, just seeking more information. I did test-drive a couple of cars. At one dealership I was confronted by a very pushy salesperson. He told me that the special financing was going to expire "anytime" and that I really ought to buy the car "today." He asked, "What do I have to do to get you to sign on the dotted line today?" The more he pushed, the more I was certain I would not be buying my new car from this man. Sometimes the unchurched perceive preachers and their altar calls in this same way.

Most of you reading this book likely do not *ever* have altar calls—they are seen as something of an anachronism in many mainline churches. We have viewed with critical eyes the use of this form of invitation in more conservative churches and, unfortunately, we have "thrown out the baby with the bathwater." We have often assumed that people will simply become Christians by osmosis if they sit under our teaching long enough. We take comfort in the fact that we ask certain vows at membership that sound like a Christian commitment, but if the truth be told, many of those who accept our membership vows have not yet really made a Christian commitment. And many of those who are ready to make a Christian commitment are not yet convinced they need the church or church membership.

Returning to our car salesman metaphor, I visited another car dealer that same Saturday morning who was so "laid-back," I had to pry information from her. My wife told me she had been to the same dealership a month before, very interested in a certain car, and the woman didn't ask if she wanted a test drive, nor did she offer more information—not even her business card. She called us a few days after our visit but still did not ever try to convince us that her vehicle was the right car, or that she could offer us a good deal. Needless to say, we did not buy our car from her, though she was much more relaxed than the first salesman.

It is important for preachers to help people actually make a commitment to Christ. At times we all need a clear invitation with a simple plan for acting upon our commitment. This is the value of the altar call. It is a call for action and commitment. At Church of the Resurrection we seldom ask people to come forward for an altar call. Instead, about once every four to six weeks I extend an invitation at the end of my sermon. I invite people to bow their heads and close their eyes. I then say something like this: "You may be here today and feel moved by this service—perhaps you've never actually told Jesus Christ that you would like to be one of his disciples. Maybe you're in need of his forgiveness and grace today, and you would like to be made clean and whole. The first step in the Christian life is simply to acknowledge your desire to belong to Christ, and your acceptance of what he has done for you. If you would like to take that step today, to commit your life to him, join me in saying this prayer—you may use your own words, or say quietly under your breath those I am about to pray . . ." And then I lead them, line by line and very slowly, in a prayer that sounds something like this: "Dear Lord, I would like to be one of your disciples. I would like to follow you. I accept the forgiveness and mercy you offer me. Wash me clean and make me new. Help me to follow you as I commit myself to you. I pray this to you, and in your name, Jesus. Amen."

I vary this prayer depending on the sermon content. One thing I have discovered is that many people need someone to actually lead them in a prayer like this. Recently a sixty-five-year-old man told me he had been attending church his whole life, but only on that day did he finally feel he had committed his life to Christ and experienced Christ's presence. He may have been a follower of Christ for years, but something happened to him as he finally made the commitment official.

We do not require people to raise their hands or to come forward. They are welcome to do this after the service. In our new building we will have a small prayer chapel where those who would like to pray with a pastor following a worship service may gather for prayer. We believe this prayer can happen simply as one prays quietly in their seat.

There are two other ways in which we invite people to make this commitment. We offer the Eucharist every Monday evening at a special service and then the first weekend of the month. As a part of our communion liturgy we explain that receiving the bread and wine is a tangible way to invite Christ into one's life, and then I help persons understand how they might pray, following the reception of the elements, in order to commit their lives to Christ. We invite our congregation to come forward to receive communion, and thus the opportunity is present for persons to kneel at the altar railings for prayer as they make their commitment to Christ.

Finally, we invite persons who are interested in joining the church to attend a "Coffee with the Pastor" (see my book *Leading Beyond the Walls* [Abingdon, 2002] for more information about our evangelism programs at COR). As part of our joining service, at the end of the coffee we invite persons to commit their lives to Christ by joining first in the Apostles' Creed, and then we lead them in a prayer of commitment.

I am persuaded that it is important to give people an opportunity to make a specific response to Christ's invitation to "come and follow me." At the same time, I believe many churches who routinely offer "altar calls" do so in a way that alienates some of the very people they wish to reach. I've outlined our solution to this twofold dilemma at the Church of the Resurrection. You will no doubt find your own way.

Following on the heels of our "fishing expedition" sermons, we turn to sermon series aimed at taking our members and new Christians deeper in their walk with Christ. Let's turn now to this, the second goal of our preaching.

GOING DEEPER

The ultimate goal of the Church of the Resurrection is to help people become deeply committed Christians. There are a host of ministries that all play a part in this. We tell our new members that they will not become a deeply committed Christian simply by attending worship—they must get involved in a small group or some other vehicle for personal spiritual growth. But, having said that, my sermons should also be helping move people in this direction.

Discipleship

You have seen in the last chapter that even our "fishing expedition" sermons seek to take people to a deeper place in their walk with Christ. In a sense, discipleship is a chief aim of every sermon. But at various times of the year we offer sermon series focused on providing tools to help worshipers grow in their understanding of the Christian faith, the Bible, or the spiritual disciplines. Lent is one of these times every year when we offer sermons that are first and foremost about growing deeper. We choose Lent as the time for such sermons for several reasons. First, historically this has been a season for preparing new believers for baptism and profession of faith in the church. It is the time when we conduct confirmation with our young people. Lent is a season, theologically, where we prepare our hearts for Good Friday and Easter, joining Jesus in forty days of fasting and prayer. In addition, following the fishing expedition series, we find that both our members and those new to the church are ready to focus on the spiritual life.

A dichotomy is sometimes seen between "seeker"-oriented sermons and "believer"-oriented sermons. We have wrestled with this same issue and considered offering some kind of "believers" service during the week. We will likely do this in the future to provide an opportunity for a longer period of praise and worship. But having said that, I think we currently have done a pretty good job of covering a wide spectrum of needs and levels of spiritual maturity in most of our sermons and sermon series. The two exceptions to this are Christmas Eve and Easter when we focus, year after year, on the simple message of these holidays and their significance in our lives. We make no bones about the fact that the sermons on these two holy days are for the unchurched. But on most weekends in worship my hope is that those who are believers are learning something new and hearing the challenge of God for their lives, while the new Christians and not-yet Christians are growing and being challenged as well.

I have been asked to preach in the style of some of the great expository Bible preachers of the past—a verse-by-verse exposition of a particular book of the Bible. I am amazed when some of our laypeople request this, as though this were giving them "meat." Here is where a "believers service" would be helpful, but I have not considered this the work of week-in and week-out preaching. I actually enjoy doing this kind of teaching when given the chance, but I have resisted this form of preaching for several reasons.

First, I do not see it modeled by Jesus or the apostles in their preaching and teaching. They were much more concerned with the practical application of spiritual truths, and with outlining spiritual principles to meet the needs of their hearers than verse-by-verse expositions of the Hebrew Scriptures.

Second, there are 31,173 verses in the entire Bible. If I were to preach every week for the next thirty years of my ministry, I would be able to preach on less than 5 percent of these verses. I feel my calling as a preacher is not unlike what I once heard a dean say was the purpose of the seminary. My seminary education was not meant to teach me everything there was to know about the Bible and theology, church history and ethics, pastoral care or preaching. My professors were no doubt constantly frustrated because they had so much more knowledge than they could possible convey to us in three or four years of study. But their goal was not to teach us everything, but to give us tools and a basic foundation that would allow us to spend the rest of our lives learning, growing, exploring, and then ministering.

I believe this is our aim as pastors—not to teach everything there is to know about any given topic, theme or book of the Bible, but to lay a foundation and provide the tools and model the methodology that would allow those entrusted to us to spend the rest of their lives exploring the Scriptures and the spiritual disciplines so that they are continually growing "in the grace and knowledge of our Lord and Savior Jesus Christ."

In my preaching then, even in the discipleship-focused series of sermons, my aim is to take a broad brush and focus on larger chunks of text or major ideas, and then to challenge our people to dig even deeper on their own. What I will share with you in this chapter are some of the sermon series we have done over the last few years aimed at taking people deeper. I will end by offering you a tool I am both proud of and excited about, which can help your members take your sermons, not as an ending point, but as a jumping-off place to go deeper in their faith.

The Man Paul

Over the last few years I have tended to choose a major theme for the year when it comes to discipleship sermons. This theme will then be divided between two sermon series—one in the spring and one in the fall. I have already mentioned several times the series of sermons on the letters of Paul. In 2000, while I was on my sermon planning retreat, I realized that I had never really taught our congregation about Paul. We had studied some of the epistles. We had preached on a story here and there from Acts, but never in the ten years the church had been in existence at that point, had we focused on Paul. The need to do so was confirmed one day when my strong-willed teenage daughter and I were talking about Paul and she said, "Paul was a sexist pig!" I was a bit taken aback. But I realized my daughter associated Paul primarily with scriptures limiting the role of women in the church. And though she had been in Sunday school and Bible study, she had not yet been able to see a comprehensive picture of this most remarkable man. I was also struck by the fact that there were likely many in our church who only knew Paul as the man who wrote that "the women were to keep silent in the church." So, in the summer of 2000 I planned to devote two sermon series in 2002 to Paul. The first series, during Lent, would introduce our congregation to "The Life and Journeys of Paul," and it would be based primarily on the second half of the Acts of the Apostles. The second series, following my own tour of the cities where Paul preached, would be "The Letters of Paul."

To be sure, these sermons did not have the drawing power of a fishing expedition. Yet the congregation knew that not only would they grow in their understanding of the Bible, and be given tools to better read and explore the Bible on their own, but each week there would be a practical, relevant, and important life application. I must admit these kind of series are the ones I most enjoy preparing for. As I noted in an earlier chapter, my aim is that the informational part of each sermon in the series be comparable to a college-level course offered on the topic. This means that my sermon reading and research time is devoted to growing deeper in my own understanding of the faith. What a wonderful joy as a pastor to be paid to spend five to ten hours doing in-depth Bible study each week in preparation for sermons like this!

I had taken many courses on Paul and been in many Bible studies on the letters of Paul, but never had I spent as much time studying this leading apostle and his work. I was able to gain insights I'd never had before. Each week I had two to three hours' worth of available material and experienced the challenge and frustration of cutting it down to the thirty minutes I would actually be able to preach.

Enough on Paul. Allow me to walk you through some of the other sermons that we've focused on aimed at taking our people deeper.

Capital Campaigns

In my sermon planning retreat in 1999 I was looking ahead to 2000 and 2001, and realizing that during this time we would be preparing for a capital campaign in the spring of 2002, to raise money for our next building. Our members would be called upon to sacrifice at a level they had never experienced before. I began to ask myself, "Are they ready for this? Have I laid a sufficient foundation in their faith? What is their level of commitment to Jesus Christ?" This prompted me to look at 2000 and 2001 as a time in which I would be most intentional about laying a solid foundation for them—putting all the pieces together in their faith.

Understanding Jesus

In 2000 I felt led to focus two series of sermons on the life, work, and teaching of Jesus Christ. Every sermon I preach is about Jesus in some way, but during this series I wanted to help our members come to love Jesus Christ—to understand the Lord's heart, his mission, his teachings, his death and resurrection, and the implications of all of these for our lives as we call him Savior and Lord.

During the season of Lent I planned a series of sermons entitled, "Portraits of Jesus from the Gospel of Luke." We invited members to read the entire Gospel of Luke while I preached on eight passages from this Gospel, which compellingly describes Jesus' heart for people. In each sermon I hoped to help our congregation members grow in their love for Christ, while also allowing their hearts to be shaped by Christ's own heart for people.

In the fall we came back with a series of sermons entitled, "Sermons on the Narrow Path: The Teachings of Jesus for Today's World." These sermons were drawn from Matthew's Gospel, and once again I invited the congregation to read through the entire Gospel of Matthew with me. During that year, then, those who took the challenge read the Gospels of both Matthew and Luke, and they came to know Jesus' ministry and his teachings. These series represented only two of the seven sermon series we offered that year—but they were designed to lay a foundation in Christian discipleship for those who were new believers while taking longtime Christians deeper in their walk with Christ.

Christian Belief

In 2001 my focus for Lent was on laying a foundation of Christian belief. I wanted to offer our congregation the equivalent of a basic course in systematic theology, Christian apologetics or, perhaps more simply, a confirmation class for the entire congregation. That year, then, we focused on "What Christians Believe and Why." I used a basic systematic theology course outline for the eight weeks of sermons.

I want to share with you one experience from that series of sermons. One week I preached on the meaning of baptism. We baptize people every week at the church—and each week I explain a bit about what baptism means. I had included references to baptism many times in sermons. But this sermon was about the history and theological significance of baptism. During part of the sermon I used slides of ancient baptismal fonts that have been discovered by archaeologists. I both taught and preached about baptism, using this sermon as an opportunity to invite people who had never been baptized, and were ready to take on all that this means, to receive the promises of God in baptism. We gave an opportunity, following the service, for persons to sign up to be baptized at our Easter Vigil baptismal service (we have a special baptismal service the night before Easter to baptize those who have never been baptized). In response to the sermon, 140 people signed up to be baptized the following Saturday evening at the vigil! These were not rebaptisms (United Methodist Churches typically don't rebaptize, but instead renew one's baptism); these were people who had never been baptized but wished to be now that they understood the significance of this act. We had two baptismal stations and baptized for more than two hours at the vigil that year! It was very, very powerful. Many of these folks had been coming to church for a long time, and despite regular references to baptism, had never felt the call to take that step until this sermon and the invitation that followed it.

Spiritual Disciplines

I'll give just a few more examples of our "Discipleship" sermon series. Generally, every two or three years I use our Lenten series as an opportunity to teach on the spiritual disciplines and how to practice them. One among my favorite series in this vein was entitled, "The Ten Habits of Highly Effective Christians"—tagging onto the plethora of books using the "highly effective" idea. Each week we would teach about, and then invite our members to practice, the various spiritual disciplines. My hope was to offer in sermon form something akin to Richard Foster's *Celebration of Discipline*. The sermons were not drawn from that text, though at several points I referred to his work.

Biblical Characters

I have often found the study of biblical characters, like Jesus and Paul, is among my favorite approaches to discipleship sermons. Among the most enjoyable for me was a series entitled, "Insights for Living from the Life of David." The following paragraph was used to describe this series of sermons in our newsletter:

King David is hailed as the greatest king Israel ever knew. His story crosses three books of the Old Testament. More than this, David's story is a powerful picture of how faith and life intersect. In his story we learn about friendship and betrayal, temptation and grace, sin and redemption, cowardice and courage, arrogance and humility, and ultimately, about the role of faith in a life well lived.

You can catch a feeling for the content of this series by looking at the sermon titles, coupled with the scripture and theme (note that May 14 was Mother's Day, and June 11 was Father's Day):

April 30	The Unlikely People God Chooses: David the Shepherd Boy	1 Samuel 16
May 7	Slaying the Giants in Your Life: David and Goliath	1 Samuel 17
May 14	A Grandmother's Legacy: David's Grandmother Ruth	Ruth
May 21	When You are Stabbed in the Back: David and Saul	1 Samuel 18
May 28	The Characteristics of True Friendship: David and Jonathon	1 Samuel 19
June 4	"What a Tangled Web We Weave": David's Affair with Bathsheba	2 Samuel 11
June 11	Problem Children and Struggling Parents: David and His Rebellious Sons	1 Kings 1
June 18	"The Lord Is My Shepherd . . .": David and His Poetry	Psalm 23
June 25	David's Last Words: David and His Legacy	1 Kings 2

As mentioned before, for most of our sermon series we produce full-color postcards announcing the series and giving the topics and dates (see the enclosed DVD for samples). With fishing expedition sermons we will mail the postcard to everyone on our mailing list. With discipleship sermon series we will often mail the postcards only to our members. The postcard is meant to create excitement about the upcoming sermons.

Sermon Notes and Study Guides

Before leaving this theme of sermons that take our parishioners deeper in their faith, I would like to share with you an invaluable tool we have developed to help our people carry the sermon with them into the coming week.

Many of you already offer sermon outlines or sermon notes—an insert in the bulletin to help members take notes so they can remember and further reflect on the sermon. This is not a new idea. I will pass on one idea for improving sermon outlines or sermon notes—and this idea came from my mother, who is a member of our church. We usually have "fill in the blank" spaces in the outline where worshipers can complete a sentence or idea in the sermon outline. My mom noted that often she was so focused on listening to the message that she missed the word. Sometimes she stopped following along in the outline altogether and then she had nowhere to find the words that were to fill in the blanks. She suggested printing the words that fill in the blanks in small print at the bottom of the page. Who am I to argue with my mother? We started doing this and people expressed appreciation—clearly others had struggled with this as well!

But the big idea I would share with you is that of our Study Guide. Some years ago I was struck by two important ideas. First, many of our people were not reading the Bible on their own. When I asked them why they were not studying their Bible they told me that when they tried to read it, they could not understand it. The second idea that moved me toward producing Study Guides was the fact that, as I mentioned earlier, I would like to include far more material in a sermon than I have time to preach. So I began to bring these two ideas together. What if I were to prepare a daily devotional that went along with the sermon?

What if I assigned scripture readings and then gave helpful hints and comments to help beginners to understand the text and apply it to their lives?

That was the beginning of the Study Guide. During the series of sermons on the life of Paul, the study guides allowed me to take our members through the entire second half of the book of Acts, freeing me from the need to cover every detail of Paul's life. During the sermons on the letters of Paul, we invited the entire congregation to read the letter I'd just preached on during the week following the sermon. I emphasized each week that the sermon was incomplete without our parishioners actually taking the Study Guide home and reading the epistle.

Each week, after I have finished writing my sermon, I spend about an hour writing the Study Guide. Last year we took a survey on Sunday morning to find out how many people actually used the Study Guides—56 percent of our people indicated using them either daily or regularly. Fifty-six percent of the congregation are studying the Bible and taking the sermons a step further! This is a valuable tool for taking people deeper in their faith. We have families who use them for their evening devotions, Sunday school classes that have occasionally followed a sermon series and used them for outlines for their class, and members who have led Bible studies in their workplace using these guides.

One last word on the Study Guides—we upload them to our Web site each week so our members who are out of town can download them, wherever they are, and can use them to pursue their own devotional time with them. If you are interested in seeing our Study Guides, simply log on to our Web site at www.cor.org! You will also find samples on the enclosed DVD.

Scripture Memorization

One spiritual discipline that many churches have ignored over the last few decades is scripture memorization. There was a time when in my own denomination, among Methodist people, this was routinely practiced. But seldom do we pastors challenge our members in this way today. During our sermons on the letters of Paul, we prepared scripture memory verse cards—choosing one key verse from each of Paul's letters. Each week these were included in the bulletin, and I invited our members to read the verses out loud twice during the service. I challenged them to place the cards on the dash of their car or somewhere else where they would have to see them daily, and commit to memorizing the scriptures. I was amazed at the number of our members and visitors who actually memorized each verse. At the beginning of worship each week I would invite those who memorized the verses to join me in repeating them—it was a real treat to see and hear how many had committed these verses to heart.

Are you leading your congregation members to a deeper understanding of the Scriptures, of Christian theology, of Jesus Christ? Are you helping them know how to practice the spiritual disciplines? Are you giving them the tools they need to become deeply committed Christians? And are you challenging them to go deeper in their faith? This is the role of discipleship sermons.

As we reach new persons for Christ and help them to become deeply committed Christians, we can never forget our role as shepherds and pastors of the flock. Let's turn now to the sermons we preach to care for the flock.

CHAPTER NINE

CARING FOR THE FLOCK

Pastoral Care

When Church of the Resurrection was a small congregation I had the joy of being the only pastor of our flock. It was a privilege to know everyone by name, to officiate at every wedding and every funeral, and to make every hospital call. I averaged just a few hospital calls a week in our early days as a congregation. We had six to eight weddings and four to six funerals per year in the first few years. But even then I would have eight to ten pastoral counseling sessions per week with members.

Most of my "counseling" load was related to marital issues, though some dealt with depression, suicide, grief, addiction, anxiety, and more. As our church grew, so did my awareness of the pain, challenges, and difficulties facing many in our congregation. We invited our members to return prayer request cards through the offering plate each week. As I read and prayed over these cards, I was given a snapshot of the pastoral care needs of the congregation. I remember feeling overwhelmed by the task of providing one-on-one care for all of these people.

Fortunately we added pastors, developed lay pastoral care ministries, and expanded our capacity to care for our congregation. Even so, it was clear to me that most people who had pastoral care needs would never make an appointment with a pastor or, by the time they did, they were in a crisis. I came to see that each week sitting in the sanctuary during worship were people struggling with pastoral care issues, and the sermon may be the only vehicle to reach them. I recognized that preaching on pastoral care related issues was not a matter of offering "feel good" sermons bordering on "pop psychology" as some pastors had told me. The needs of the congregation were serious, and my job as pastor was to seek to care for the flock entrusted to me.

Relationships

I have already mentioned the sermon series I preached entitled "Biblical Perspectives on Love, Marriage, and Sex." I will likely rewrite and preach this series of sermons once every five to six years. The sheer number of people who turned out for this "fishing expedition/pastoral care" series of sermons pointed to the tremendous hunger people have for improving their relationships with the opposite sex. The surveys we conducted for the series on relationships pointed out that, while there were many wonderful marriages in the congregation, there were also a large number of persons who experienced pain in this part of their lives. I believe Christianity holds the key to helping persons live in relationships that bless and build up, rather than wound and tear down. Following Christ, and living the gospel, forces us to move from self-centeredness to sacrificial love. Furthermore, I found that many young people have not grown up with effective role models for healthy relationships, but neither have they learned about relationships in the church. Today, many learn about dating, love, marriage, and sex from the television or movies. Pastors have a responsibility to preach and teach on these issues.

Suicide

But marital issues are not the only pastoral care needs we must address from the pulpit. On any given weekend in your congregation, there will be persons who have contemplated suicide in the past week. Several years ago, I preached a sermon on suicide. This sermon was prompted by a rash of suicides in our community among area middle school and high school students, including one young man in our own congregation. My aim in this sermon was to address this concern not only among those in worship, but, through the recorded copy of this tape to provide a resource for our church members to share with their friends or family members who were contemplating suicide. The audiotape of this sermon is always available at our tape ministry.

Most often the pastoral care sermons I offer will be nestled within other sermon series. It is not uncommon for my sermons to address at least one pastoral care issue, even when the sermon itself has another focus. In the remainder of this chapter I will offer a few examples of pastoral care sermons I have preached and key points to remember as you provide care for your flock through preaching.

The Problem of Evil

Among the most important pastoral care needs in your congregation are those related to the theological and spiritual issues surrounding the problem of evil. Even the most committed Christians will struggle with faith questions when faced with tragedy. I have found that I must address issues related to suffering and faith at least four times each year. If individuals cannot work through the issues related to suffering in a healthy way, despair, anxiety, and depression can result. Congregants need their pastors to help them understand how and why they should put their trust in God when their friends are dying of cancer, or children are killed in automobile accidents, or terrorist events claim the lives of thousands of innocent people.

Mortality

If you can provide meaningful and helpful ways to attempt to make sense of tragedy and suffering, you will have already played a key role in shepherding your flock. In addition to these questions, our role as pastors is to offer consolation and hope in the face of death. As human beings we naturally wrestle with our own mortality. More often we struggle with the grief and loss of others we love. Every week several of my congregants lose parents. In an average year, three to five families in our church will lose children under the age of eighteen. Nearly everyone will know someone who died during the year. Death is a constant factor in our lives. As pastors we serve a risen Lord, and we are called to remind people of the hope we have in Christ.

In recent years pastors in mainline and more liberal traditions looked down upon the hope of eternal life as an unsophisticated theological concept. I well remember one of my Systematic Theology professors in seminary teaching that he did not believe in heaven or an afterlife. Yet what a tragedy to deny one of the central doctrines of the Christian faith, and the most life-giving of our tenets! I believe it was C. S. Lewis who once said, "Nothing affects how we live more than what we believe about death." Thus one of the most important issues we can address in providing pastoral care to our congregations is also at the very heart of the gospel we proclaim—that there is hope beyond this life, that "when this mortal life is through we have a building, not made by human hands, eternal in the heavens"; that "neither death nor life, nor angels nor demons, nor things present, nor things to come . . . can separate us from the love of God in Christ Jesus our Lord"; that Jesus is the "resurrection and the life. Those who believe in him will never die."

For Teens

In addition to these primary concerns, I have offered, on two occasions in recent years, series of sermons that were focused on the pastoral care needs of teens. In these sermons I surveyed our youth group and Sunday school programs to discover the issues they wrestled with. I then invited a group of teens to meet with me weekly as an advisory group to talk through the issues, sharing their insights and ideas as I was preparing the messages. What became apparent in each sermon was that the issues we face as youth do not go away when we become adults—they simply take on different forms. Most adults I know still wrestle with issues related to their parents. Many struggle with alcohol and drug problems. Sex and temptation continue to be part of our lives as adults. Swearing, anger, suicide, depression—all these issues plague adults as well as kids. Thus each sermon allowed me to begin by talking about and to teens, but before the sermons were over the message had shifted to address the needs of our adults as well.

Other topics I have covered in pastoral care sermons in the last couple of years have included:

Anxiety Disorders and Panic Attacks
Sexual Abuse by Clergy and Others
Learning How to Forgive
Internet Pornography
Aging
Rape

There have been too many others to mention. Again, many of these are within the context of a sermon that is focused on an altogether different topic.

Hands-On Pastoral Care

One last word about pastoral care sermons: Not only do they require doing extraordinary exegetical work and a good deal of homework in the mental health field, but to be effective at preaching these sermons a pastor must continue to be involved in direct pastoral care with parishioners. Those pastors in smaller churches are by necessity involved in hands-on pastoral care. But those of us serving large churches typically have a staff of people serving in the pastoral care department. When this is the case. it is all the more important that you as a pastor continue to set aside time each month for meeting with people who are struggling and in need of pastoral care. I typically meet with four to six people per week in need of pastoral care. I continue to make a handful of hospital calls each month because *I need this* in order to be an effective pastor and preacher.

None of us are simply "preachers." We all are called to be pastors—to offer the healing, hope, love, and grace that Christ extends to his children. Pastoral care sermons are among the most important messages we will share.

Evangelism, discipleship, and pastoral care form the foundation for creating healthy congregations and Christians. But the Christian faith is always more than a calling simply to appropriate the blessings of God for ourselves. We are always "blessed to be a blessing," which leads us to sermons that equip and inspire the flock to take their faith into the world.

CHAPTER TEN

PREPARING GOD'S PEOPLE TO DO THE WORK OF THE MINISTRY

When it comes to our work as preachers, Ephesians 4:11-12 is among the most important passages of Scripture in the New Testament: "The gifts he gave were that some would be apostles, some prophets, some evangelists, some pastors and teachers, to equip the saints for the work of ministry, for building up the body of Christ."

Equipping and Sending

We are called to equip the laity for the work of the ministry. Committed Christians will serve God with their time. They will minister to one another in the church. They will pursue acts of justice and mercy in the world. They will share their faith with others. They will live as salt and light. And this is where Equipping and Sending sermons are important. These are sermons you intentionally plan to preach every year that will guide your members to understand God's call on their lives and to pursue those things that will prepare them for this task. More than that, these sermons are designed to inspire your people to do whatever it takes to pursue God's mission for their lives, for the church, and for the world.

Once again, it is likely that these sermons will appear in many of your series on discipleship. Sometimes an entire series of sermons will be both Discipleship and Equipping and Sending. But while every sermon should have a way to respond to the Word, Equipping and Sending sermons will offer a very specific call to action and they will come with the conviction that each person should respond. Allow me to give a few examples.

Sharing Faith

At Church of the Resurrection our members are excellent at inviting their friends to church. But most are not as comfortable actually talking about their faith with another. So, several years ago I preached a sermon to teach them how to share their faith with a friend. I included in the bulletin an insert they could take home, which answered several simple questions designed to help them articulate the difference Christ had made in their lives, and then how to invite someone else to follow Christ. The final step was to challenge them to consider a friend they wanted to pray for and begin finding ways to share Christ with them.

Spiritual Gifts

As part of our emphasis on equipping our members for ministry, we taught about the gifts of the Holy Spirit, inviting our members to discover their spiritual gifts. We showed video testimonials of persons who had been through our Spiritual Gifts Discovery Course (available through Abingdon Press as *Serving from the Heart*) describing the impact this course had on their spiritual lives. Then, as part of our Study Guide, we included a short version of the questionnaire used in the class, both to pique the interest of our worshipers so they would sign up for the course and to help those who wouldn't sign up to begin to discover their gifts.

Spiritual Growth

As I noted earlier, each year we preach a series of sermons aimed at reminding our congregation about their membership vows and inspiring them to step up their involvement and commitment both to spiritual growth opportunities and to ministry opportunities within and outside the walls of the church. In 2002 this was done through a series of sermons our pastors shared in called, "Unleashing the Power of the Laity." Each week a sermon focused on a different opportunity to grow and serve and included a biblical foundation, a challenge, video testimonials of those involved in these ministries, and a concrete opportunity to respond. These sermons are often accompanied by a "Mission Fair" in which we invite mission agencies in Kansas City to set up booths in our narthex with information about their ministry and their current need for volunteers. The response to the sermon is to go to the narthex and find one area in which to volunteer and serve in the coming year. We've taken a similar approach to the various ministry opportunities within the life of our church. A complete listing of the most pressing ministry needs is included in the bulletin each week.

Current Events

One of the more intriguing series of sermons we have done was a series aimed at discipleship as well as equipping and sending:

"The Gospel and the Stories Making News Today." I referred to this series briefly in chapter 5. Our aim was to help Church of the Resurrection worshipers reflect on the stories in the evening news in light of their faith—to understand that nearly every newscast is filled with opportunities for Christians to live out their faith.

My hope in this series was to teach our parishioners how to do Christian ethics, how to think about contemporary issues, and how to listen for God's call. In each of these sermons we gave a specific opportunity for our members to respond. As I noted earlier, this series was produced in partnership with the news department of our local ABC affiliate, KMBC. Each Monday morning our worship planning team would consider a list of local news stories from the prior week and select one story for the sermon that weekend. KMBC would then provide their news graphics, any footage of the news story they used (and some they didn't use), and together we would write a script for their anchors to read from the news desk. This two-minute opening formed the jumping-off point for each sermon. You will find the promo we produced for this series, which we showed on Easter morning, on the DVD included with this book. I'd like to devote the rest of this chapter to describing a few of the specific sermons in this series.

The Public School System

The series opened with what had been the top news story for months in Kansas City—but which had reached a crescendo the week of this sermon. The Kansas City, Missouri, public school system, with thirty-four thousand students, was in trouble. Earlier in the year it had become the first major school system in America to have its accreditation revoked by a State Board of Education. Reeling from this, the six thousand employees of the district were struggling with morale issues. The week of this sermon the superintendent of schools was fired by the local school board, was reinstated by a federal judge, and then resigned. He was the seventeenth superintendent of schools in twenty-three years. The district was once again in chaos.

The community in which our church is located is in the suburbs on the Kansas side of the Kansas City area. It has one of the top-rated school systems in America. People move to our area for the schools. Our area is the result of a "white flight" that began in the 1960s when neighborhoods and schools in the urban core began to be integrated. Most of our members were only children during that time, and they neither remember this nor understand it.

We opened the sermon on that day with the questions: "Does God care about the thirty-four thousand students in the Kansas City, Missouri, school district who are struggling to receive a good education? Does God care about the six thousand plus teachers, administrators, and staff of the school system? And is there something God would call us to do in response to this crisis?" In the sermon I went on to outline the historic commitment Methodists have had to public education. Interestingly enough, the public schools in Kansas City, Missouri, were started in the basement of the Westport Methodist Church by a Methodist preacher. Likewise, the first schools on the Kansas side of the state line in Kansas City were started as part of the Methodist mission to the Shawnee Indians.

After looking at the scriptures that motivated those early Methodists to start schools for children, we looked at what action we as a church could take to be used by God to encourage and bring healing to our urban core schools. I challenged our teachers to consider leaving the suburban school districts they served in and offer their services in the urban core (we had teachers who did this). We challenged our teenagers to consider answering God's call to be urban schoolteachers. And then we ended the sermon by passing the offering plates (we had collected the offering earlier in the service). People assumed we were taking a second offering, but instead of asking people to put money in the plates, we invited them to take something out of the plate. Our director of Missions and Community Outreach and his team had collected the name, position, school, and school address of every one of the more than six thousand district employees, and had placed these names on cards with specific suggestions for how our church members could bless and encourage these employees. These cards were placed in the offering plates. Every attendee that morning in worship was asked to take one card, to pray for that employee during worship, then to take the card home and send this employee a letter thanking them for their care for kids, letting them know we were praying for them, and offering help in whatever form we could give it.

As I announced this opportunity there was something of a stunned silence in the congregation. Some of our people began to cry. The cards were passed and the people began to pray. By Friday of that week stories began to pour into our offices. Our members had included their phone numbers and offered to help, and teachers were calling. That first week a handful of our members had already gone down to volunteer as assistants in the classrooms. By the next week even more had answered the call. One man got his entire company involved and adopted a school. A team from our missions department adopted another school and agreed to provide school supplies. One man organized a scholarship fund for kids. One of the other local news stations came to do a story on our church after having received calls from one of the schools describing what we had done. And all this was the result of just the first sermon!

Actually, that was the most dramatic of the sermons, but each one followed the same pattern—a news story, connecting the gospel to that story, and an invitation to respond in specific and concrete ways.

Conservation

The other stories included a story on skyrocketing gasoline prices (gas prices had risen by 50 percent during that period of time). From the opening story we spoke about what it means to be a steward of the earth, and God's ultimate claim on our planet. We looked at the relationship between discipleship and conservation and the possibility that God does care about these issues. We challenged our members with regard to the vehicles they drive, to consider seeking to improve their fuel economy by just 10 percent with the next vehicle they purchase. We ran the math using EPA formulas and found that with the number of members in our congregation, if each one improved their fuel economy by 10 percent—that's simply moving from an average economy of 17 miles per gallon on their current vehicle (estimated based on the mix of SUVs to automobiles in our church parking lot) to 18.7 miles per gallon on their next vehicle—as a congregation we would save 222,000 gallons of gasoline per year! And we would produce 4,500,000 pounds less CO_2 emissions! To lead the way, LaVon and I traded in our Honda CRV sport utility vehicle that averaged about 20 miles per gallon for a Honda Insight hybrid electric car that has an EPA average fuel economy of 64 miles per gallon. We parked the car on the island in front of the main entrance to the church, and I concluded the sermon by inviting our members to consider reducing fuel use by 10 percent either by conservation or by purchasing a car that averaged just 10 percent better mileage than their current car. Eighteen months later a group of clergy would organize a campaign asking Americans, "What Would Jesus Drive?" Our members were proud that we had addressed this issue a year and a half earlier.

Not everyone was pleased with these sermons. The sermon on the connection between faith and the environment prompted some to think I had lost my mind! I received several angry e-mails from folks who thought this was not a topic worthy of a sermon. I received many more from those who were encouraged by this. In a subsequent sermon I was able to reiterate what I will tell you here—that the very point of this sermon series was to demonstrate that being a disciple of Jesus Christ has implications for every part of our lives, including our consumption of resources and what we do with the planet we live on. I wanted our members to look at every news story and say, "I wonder what being a Christian has to do with that?"

The Cost of Discipleship

Another story was that of Kansas missionaries Martin and Gracia Burnham, who were captured by rebels in the Philippines (Martin was later killed, but Gracia escaped imprisonment). We spoke of the cost of discipleship, what it might mean to serve Christ in mission to the world, and what price we would be willing to pay to be counted as a disciple of Jesus Christ.

War

The week before Memorial Day in 2001 the big news, locally and nationally, was the fiftieth anniversary of Pearl Harbor, and the interest in this was being fanned by the release of the Hollywood motion picture *Pearl Harbor*. We were able to obtain footage of the film before it was released. The opening news story followed those that had been in the news every day that week about the fiftieth anniversary of the Japanese attack on Pearl Harbor. This provided the opportunity to explore the entire idea of war and, in particular, the theory of just war. In this sermon we interviewed two retired United Methodist pastors in our congregation—one who was an Air Force pilot in World War II and one who was a conscientious objector assigned to civil service during the war. The only call for action in this sermon came in its conclusion—four months *before* September 11, 2001:

> You may be asking why you should care about these issues of when, or if, war is ever justified. You may be thinking, *Why is this the topic of a sermon?* But the ideas related to just war were worked out in the church, and by theologians, to help Christians wrestle with when the use of force is justified. And I can assure you today that the day will come, sometime in the next few years, when we will be faced with these very issues as a nation. And you will need to know what you believe as a Christian about war. Because it will be some of you, and your sons and your daughters who will be called upon to fight.

After the attack on America in September 2001, there were hundreds of requests for this tape, and the issue of just war continued to be in the news throughout 2002 and beyond.

Misconceptions About Retirement

The last of the stories we focused on in this series of sermons was an uplifting news story about a woman named Audrey Stewart, who had just celebrated her 105th birthday. At 105 she was still working part-time, proofing stories at a local newspaper! Her comments about her life and her work were the perfect starting point to talk about Americans' misconceptions about retirement. So many in our congregation speak of retiring when they are in their fifties or early sixties, with plans to play golf and travel the world. My challenge to our members was to rethink what it means to retire. Retirement simply means you no longer have to work for a paycheck—which means now there are no excuses as to why you can't serve God with more of your time! We spoke of the tragedy of a gifted person's retiring at age fifty-five and spending the rest of their life focused on hitting a little white ball around in the grass. And we spoke of the call of God on our lives, which doesn't stop when we hit fifty-five or sixty-five or seventy-five. From here we jumped into the scriptures to look at the stories of those who had the greatest impact for the kingdom of God, and their ages. Abraham and Sarah were in their nineties when God called them. Moses was past retirement when he led the Israelites out of slavery. Elijah, too, was an old man when he did battle with the prophets of Baal. Paul was in his fifties and sixties when he wrote nearly half the books of the New Testament. And John was likely in his eighties or nineties when he wrote the five books attributed to his name. Throughout history, some of the most prolific Christian leaders were past the midpoint of their lives. The challenge in the sermon was to ask our members, as they are making plans for their retirement, to rethink what they plan to do when they retire. It is fine to go play a little golf and to travel a bit—but it may very well be that our finest and most productive years for the Kingdom will come after we retire.

Although I've probably told you far more about each of these sermons than was needed, my hope is to encourage you to think about how you can equip, inspire, and send your congregation members into the mission field where God has placed them, to serve God and have an impact for God's kingdom.

CHAPTER ELEVEN

SERMONS TO STRENGTHEN THE CHURCH

I n this chapter we come to the last of the five aims I have for
my sermons. In chapter 1, I called this "Institutional
Development," though I prefer to think of these sermons as
"Sermons to Strengthen the Church." Most of the sermons I
preach are aimed at strengthening, encouraging, and equipping
worshipers. But the sermons we will speak of in this chapter are
specifically focused on the health of the church itself. These sermons will usually have a personal dimension for our members.
They will often be discipleship sermons, or sometimes equipping
and sending sermons, but they are virtually never evangelistic.
These sermons are essential to the church—if you don't preach
these sermons, your congregation will suffer in ways that are very
real but often difficult at first glance to discern.

What type of sermons am I referring to? Specifically, sermons
in which you as the leader of your church cast the vision for
where God is calling the church in the future; sermons that

address the issues facing your church in the present; and sermons in which you preach on stewardship and during which you purposefully seek to increase the operating funds to the church or raise money for buildings. If you do not preach on these issues, your church will never be the vital, healthy church it can and should be. At the same time, these sermons must be preached sparingly. Too many sermons about the church itself will create a congregation with an institutional mind-set—one that is inwardly focused.

Let's take a look at a few of the ways we have approached these delicate but important issues.

Preaching on Money

At the Church of the Resurrection we have conducted five capital funds campaigns in nine years. Three of these were directed to the entire congregation and two of them were follow-up campaigns directed at the one thousand plus members who had joined since the prior campaign was held. In addition, nearly every fall we have a special focus on stewardship of resources, which coincides with our annual pledge campaign. For most pastors, fund-raising is the least rewarding part of our work. And like many of you, I would rather preach on almost anything other than finances and stewardship. But I also know that if I cannot effectively preach and lead our congregation in these areas, we will never become the church God has called us to be. As the preaching pastor, you are the chief development officer for your church. This is part of the job.

In my book *Leading Beyond the Walls* (Abingdon, 2002), I offer more information on how we design stewardship campaigns at the church. For our present purposes, I want to mention a few principles that I have learned are essential to raising money.

First, people give to visions, not to budgets. At Church of the Resurrection we have three COR visions—what we believe God has called us to focus on for the foreseeable future. The first is to reach nonreligious and nominally religious people whom other churches may not be able to reach, and to help them become committed Christians—something you have already heard in our purpose statement. The second vision is to transform our community. Our belief is that twenty years from now the Kansas City area will be a significantly different place—the values and culture will look more like the kingdom of God—because we were here. The final vision is that God might use us as a catalyst for renewal within the mainline denominations, which were in decline throughout most of the last third of the twentieth century.

We recently completed a capital campaign in which we raised $28 million in three-year pledges to construct our next building. This campaign was conducted during the 2002 recession. We raised those funds without even having finalized the architectural drawings. We were still developing these plans during the capital campaign. But what we knew, and what our members knew, was that they were not really giving to a building. People are rarely inspired to make significant sacrifices for a building. But they will make significant sacrifices for a vision that changes the world. In our campaign the building is only a tool to help us achieve these visions—it is not the end, but a means to an end. So our sermons and our fund-raising were focused on ministry and vision, not bricks and mortar.

I remember when one of our members told me that he and his wife were committing over $200,000 to the campaign. He said, "Adam, you know we support a lot of different projects, but what really moved us to make this kind of commitment is the dream that we could actually help other churches be renewed. I attended a Lutheran church before coming to COR, and I so want to see my former denomination, and mainline churches, renewed!" He said nothing about giving to a building—he was giving to a vision.

You, as a preacher, must be able to cast the vision of how the world will be different because of the work your church could do, if only it had the resources. Your people will need to see your conviction, your passion, and your willingness to lead them in sacrifice. You cannot preach on tithing if you are not a tither. You cannot preach on sacrifice to a capital campaign, or a missions campaign, or any other special offering that you yourself are not willing to sacrifice for.

It is in the area of raising funds that stories are so important. It is essential that you be able to tell stories about real people whose lives have been or will be changed as a result of your church's efforts. Sometimes these are effectively done using video, but sometimes you are the more effective storyteller. I've seen people who had powerful stories, but they could not tell their story in a compelling way in front of a camera.

A second important element of preaching on money is *humor*—it helps if you can introduce a funny story that takes away from, or perhaps recognizes the natural discomfort we all feel about being asked for money.

A third is your conviction that tithing and stewardship are discipleship issues. In this way, the more committed your people are to Christ, and the more they long to follow the will of God, the more open they will be to sermons about giving.

Finally, know that people will complain when you preach about giving and especially when you are asking for a sacrificial commitment to help build buildings. Often those who complain the loudest are those who are uncomfortable because they don't feel they can contribute, and they feel a measure of guilt. Instead of recognizing this for what it is and accepting it—they seek to oppose the project or cause. You cannot allow these persons to dissuade you from moving forward. You should listen to these folks—if they are your key leaders, this may indicate that you haven't done your groundwork in getting your leadership on board with the project. Even if they are not your key leaders, you should listen to see if there is something important you've missed in their criticism. But once you have listened, and you are still certain you are heading in the right direction, then keep moving forward. There will always be naysayers—most are good-hearted people who lack either the vision, faith, or resources to get behind the project. Accept them and move on.

I once heard a story told by Jim Buskirk, the now retired pastor of First United Methodist Church of Tulsa, that I have enjoyed ever since. Allow me to share it, with apologies to Jim if

I have remembered some of the details incorrectly. Jim and some of his pastor friends were on a skiing trip to Colorado. They had a great cabin right at the base of one of the mountains, though the portion of the mountain behind their cabin did not have any lifts leading up it, nor any ski runs. One of the pastors looked up the mountain and said, "Hey guys, let's take our skis and hike up this mountain. The snow is virgin powder. No one has skied on it before. It won't be easy, but imagine the experience when we ski down!" Several of them chimed in and said, "Okay! Let's do it!" But Jim and one of his friends said, "You guys are nuts! Who in their right mind carries skies and boots halfway up a mountain for just a few minutes of pleasure as you ski down? We'll stay right here by the fire and enjoy our coffee—you go right ahead and ski!"

Well, the other pastors decided they'd take the challenge. Jim and his friend watched over the next thirty minutes as these guys hiked up the side of the mountain, skis, boots, and poles slung over their shoulders. The whole way the two pastors by the fire congratulated themselves on their wisdom and spoke of the stupidity of those fellas hiking the mountain. But then they watched as these guys put on their skis and turned and began skiing where no one else had dared to ski before. As they arrived back at the cabin these other men were shouting and laughing and speaking of their great adventure. Jim said, "My friend and I could only stand there in silence as they talked of the experience with intense satisfaction. And then one of the men looked at me and said, 'Jim, you missed the very best part of our entire vacation!' "

I tell you that story, butchered though it no doubt was, because I have shared it with my own congregation on several occasions when we were facing capital campaigns. And I have said to our folks, "I know there are some of you who by nature are the types that want to sit by the fire. This project scares you. It seems too hard. You can think of a million reasons we should not pursue it. But the rest of us feel this is where God is leading. So it's okay if you don't want to go along. You can even talk about us while we're trying to scale this huge mountain. But my fear is that when we're on the back side, and we cut the ribbon on that new building, and there are thousands of people whose lives are changed as a result—and the rest of us are celebrating—my fear is that you might have missed the best part."

One more word about fund-raising. It is much easier to raise funds if your church is working toward a clear, compelling, and biblical purpose, and you can demonstrate how the funds you are raising, whether for capital or the annual ministry budget, will support the fulfillment of that purpose.

Preaching About Purpose

Let's shift gears from raising funds to a second kind of sermon you must preach to strengthen your church—sermons focused on the church's purpose. In this vein I believe Rick Warren's book *The Purpose-Driven Church* is still perhaps one of the best resources for local congregations. Warren has written the book most pastors of growing churches wish they had written. His basic premise is as old as the Bible itself—that amazing things can happen when a group of people are united around a common purpose or cause, especially when those people are empowered by the Holy Spirit and the cause is pursuing the Lord's work. Healthy churches will have a clear picture of their purpose, and it is the job of the leader to help them discover and claim this biblical mandate, and then to continually remind them of it. Warren, looking to the biblical story of Nehemiah, believes that churches must be reminded of their purpose through a sermon or some other means at least once a month.

At Church of the Resurrection I regularly refer to our purpose in the midst of a wide variety of sermons, but at least three times a year I preach a sermon specifically focused on reminding people of our purpose. Offering compelling stories both from the Bible and from our own ministry rekindle the congregation's passion around our purpose. The last time I preached a sermon on our purpose, one of our leaders came to me and said, "In my ministry area we had become cranky with one another, and we were losing a bit of our joy—we had lost sight of why we were doing this.

Your sermon rekindled our passion. I remember now why we're doing these things. And as a result of this one message I feel ready to go back and get to work!" What this woman expressed is profound in that it describes what happens to your entire congregation in the midst of serving the Lord—people get tired and cranky and tend to forget why they're doing what they're doing. It is the job of the leader to remind the people of their purpose, their biblical mandate, and to inspire the people to pursue it. As the preaching pastor of your church, you are that leader.

One final reminder about institutional development sermons: These sermons must make up right at 10 to 15 percent of the sermons you preach each year—more, or less, and your congregation will begin to lose its vitality.

CHAPTER TWELVE

IDEAS FOR ADVENT AND CHRISTMAS

E very year as I develop my sermon plans for the next twenty-four months there is always one month—one season—for which I struggle to develop sermons: December and the season of Advent. I believe it is important to focus on Advent themes during this month—to prepare my congregation to rightly celebrate Christ's birth while making themselves ready for Christ's promised return. The challenge for me is to find creative and fresh ways to approach Advent. I feel the same challenge in preparing sermons for Christmas Eve and Easter. The story is the same year after year: What new thing can be said of these events? Or what new approach can be taken that congregants haven't heard before? Combine this with the fact that these are the year's highest-attended weekends of worship, and I find this the perfect recipe for "writer's block"!

You might struggle with these same feelings, so I thought I would share with you a few ideas to help stir your own creativity for Advent and a couple of hints for preaching on Christmas Eve. I'll begin with a simple reminder about the historical background and key ideas of Advent for those readers who may not be as familiar with the liturgical year.

In the early church, Easter was the primary focal point for Christians. In preparation for it, believers fasted, prayed, and recommitted their lives to Christ. There was some certainty as to when Easter occurred because it could be traced back to the date of the Jewish Passover. Celebrating the birth of Jesus did not come into its own until perhaps the third century. At present, two different dates are used for the observance of the Christ Mass, the celebration of Christ's birth. The Orthodox observe Christmas on January 6; the Western churches (Protestant and Roman Catholic) observe Christmas on December 25. By 380 (perhaps much earlier) a fast was prescribed for priests in one region to prepare the people for the celebration of Christ's birth. This period of fasting, which was originally forty days to correspond to the forty-day fasting of Lent, was later changed to four weeks. Over time, Advent and Christmas came to be among the best-loved times of the liturgical year. They mark the beginning of the church's new year. At Church of the Resurrection, attendance at Candlelight Christmas Eve services usually, but just barely, outnumbers attendance on Easter.

The word *Advent* itself means "coming" and highlights the three primary emphases of this season each of which receives attention during this time. These three are:

1. *The prophetic promises from the Old Testament that a Davidic king would come to reign over the house of Israel forever.* During the time of the Babylonian exile of the Jews, these promises took on special significance—the exiles lived by this hope, which assured that they would return to Judah and be restored. Yet after the exile no king or leader of Judah completely fulfilled the promises of the prophets. Thus by the time of Jesus' birth the messianic expectation was still alive, and there were many who were awaiting "the consolation of Israel." Advent is a season during which we remember the prophetic promises and the longing of ancient Israel for the coming of

the "shepherd King." This emphasis of Advent is well captured in both the words and music of the hymn "O Come, O Come, Emmanuel."

2. *The events surrounding Jesus' birth—his "first coming."* Here the emphasis is on the angels who announced to Mary that she would have a child, her response to this "annunciation," and the story of Elizabeth, who gave birth to John the Baptist. Though his ministry occurred thirty years after Jesus' birth, the work of John the Baptist in preparing the way for the Lord is emphasized during Advent—an invitation for contemporary worshipers to prepare our hearts to receive the Messiah. Related to this theme of Advent are the hymns about Mary like "To a Maid Engaged to Joseph," which tells the story from Luke's Gospel of the annunciation. Also "Lo, How a Rose E'er Blooming," which speaks of prophecies that a "branch shall spring forth from Jesse" turning the branch into a rose. In this emphasis we are getting ready to once again celebrate Jesus' birth. We begin to sing Christmas carols and prepare for the holy night on which we celebrate the Savior's birth.

3. *The second coming of Christ and/or the day Christ comes for us in our death.* This is the final emphasis of Advent. Here the subject is the unfulfilled prophecies about Christ, his own promises, and those of the other New Testament writers, that Christ will one day return to usher in the new age with a new heaven and new earth. Hymns like "Marching to Zion" and "Rejoice, the Lord Is King" capture this theme, as in verse four of the latter: "Rejoice in glorious hope! Jesus the Judge shall come, and take his servants up to his eternal home. We soon shall hear the archangel's voice, the trump of God shall sound, rejoice!" The focus of this theme is on being personally prepared and ready for that day when he returns.

In addition to these three emphases, it has become traditional to ascribe to each Sunday a key word or theme. There is some inconsistency in what these four words are among the various churches. Joy is typically associated with the third Sunday—beyond this the themes may vary.

As I look back over the last ten years' Advent sermons, I find I have preached again and again on the "characters surrounding Christmas"—Joseph, Mary, the angels, the shepherds, Elizabeth, and Zechariah. I have preached on John the Baptist and his ministry. I have focused on the prophetic promises and their historical settings, which were fulfilled in an ultimate sense through Jesus Christ. I have focused on the Christian hope of the Second Coming. But over the last few years I have tried to be a bit more creative in how I approach this season.

A Christmas Carol

In 2001 we used Dickens's *A Christmas Carol* as the outline for our Advent sermons. We began Advent with a scene from the play featuring the Ghost of Christmas Past. We dimmed the lights, and a silhouetted figure in chains, who represented Scrooge's dead partner, Marley, spoke to Scrooge from the other side. We had prerecorded the following dialogue from the play:

> Then Marley, Scrooge's partner, dead now seven years, appeared before him, bound in chains.
> "You are fettered," said Scrooge, trembling. "Tell me why?"
> "I wear the chain I forged in life," replied the Ghost. "I made it link by link, and yard by yard; I girded it on of my own free will, and of my own free will I wore it. Is its pattern strange to you?"
> Scrooge trembled more and more.
> "Or would you know," pursued the Ghost, "the weight and length of the strong coil you bear yourself? It was full as heavy and as long as this seven Christmas Eves ago. You have laboured on it, since. It is a ponderous chain!"
> Scrooge glanced about him on the floor, in the expectation of finding himself surrounded by some fifty or sixty fathoms of iron cable but he could see nothing.

From this dialogue we moved into the sermon, looking at what it was that shaped Ebenezer Scrooge and how he came to be such a hard man, shackled in chains. This led us to consider the way in which each of us may be shackled—the chains we bear from the wounds of our past, the hardness of our hearts, the sins that master us, the lies we have believed. Finally, we turned to the scripture for the day—we focused on the prophetic promises of the Messiah, who would "proclaim freedom for the captives." We examined the role Jesus plays in setting us free from the chains in our lives.

Each successive week we followed a similar pattern, focusing next on the Ghost of Christmas Present and then the Ghost of Christmas Future. The scripture would be read at the conclusion of the sermon as the final "aha!" moment—pointing toward the significance of Jesus' coming for Scrooge and for us.

For the Living of These Days

During Advent of 2002 we entered once more into a partnership with the local ABC news affiliate. The sermon series title was taken from the refrain of a Harry Emerson Fosdick hymn: "For the Living of These Days: Advent 2002." Each week we focused on the top stories that shaped our nation during 2002, and then looked at how the scripture readings assigned by the Lectionary might speak to these stories. Every sermon began with the local news anchor, Larry Moore, sitting at the news desk at KMBC addressing our congregation, yet telling the news story just as he would if it had been on the nightly news.

The first week we focused on the scandals in corporate America that saw chief executives at several of the nation's top companies led away in handcuffs for accounting fraud. Twenty-six of the largest companies in America were under investigation during this year. We examined what might have caused the leading executives of these companies to act as they did. This led us to look at our own struggle with temptation and sin. Finally we turned to Isaiah 64:1-8—a psalm of lament and confession inspired by the downfall of Jerusalem. Listen to these words from the last section of this passage:

We have all become like one who is unclean, and all our right-eous deeds are like a filthy cloth. We all fade like a leaf, and our iniquities, like the wind, take us away. There is no one who calls on your name, or attempts to take hold of you; for you have hidden your face from us, and have delivered us into the hand of our iniquity. Yet, O LORD, you are our Father; we are the clay, and you are the potter; we are all the work of your hand (Isaiah 64:6-8).

This passage served as an invitation to our own members to repent, to be placed on God's potter's wheel and reshaped in preparation for celebrating Christmas. The offertory, which follows the sermon at Church of the Resurrection, was a song about being the clay in God's hands. During this song we had a potter sitting at a wheel, shaping a lump of clay into a bowl, which was then presented to God and laid upon the altar table—symbolizing the invitation to place our lives in God's hands.

Each subsequent week we examined another news story and sought to find comfort, hope, or help in the various Advent readings—which were amazingly pertinent to each story. During week two we examined the war on terrorism and the question of how we live in a day where terrorism and war are a constant threat. The answer is found in Isaiah 40:1-5, 10-11—words addressed to the Jewish exiles in Babylon who were terrorized by their captors.

In week three we focused on the stories of sexual abuse by clergy in the church. The foundations of the Roman Catholic Church were shaken in 2002. I had, the week before my sermon, invited members who had been sexually abused to write and tell me not only their stories of abuse, but how they overcame these things. Twelve members gave me their stories. That weekend's sermon focused on the problem of abusive clergy, how one moves from being a victim to being a survivor of abuse and, finally, to the passage of scripture in Isaiah 61:1-3:

The spirit of the Lord GOD is upon me, because the LORD has anointed me; he has sent me to bring good news to the oppressed, to bind up the brokenhearted, to proclaim liberty to the captives, and release to the prisoners; to proclaim the year of the LORD's favor, and the day of vengeance of our God; to comfort all who mourn; to provide for those who mourn in Zion—to give them a garland instead of ashes, the oil of glad-ness instead of mourning, the mantle of praise instead of a faint spirit. They will be called oaks of righteousness, the planting of the LORD, to display his glory.

This was a powerful passage of scripture, in its context address-ing those who had memories of abuse and years of hard labor in Babylon, now returning to Jerusalem yet bearing the old scars. Jesus reads from this passage as he preaches his first recorded ser-mon in Luke's Gospel saying, "Today this scripture is fulfilled in your hearing." The scripture offers joy to those who had mourned and promises that God will take the wounded and make them "oaks of righteousness." This was a profound word not only to those who had been abused, but to all who had ever been wounded by others.

The fourth week of Advent we took a story that was a bit lighter—the story of the midterm elections that was the focus of media attention throughout the fall of 2002. We then looked at what qualities made for an excellent elected official. For this I interviewed five persons from our congregation who currently or formerly held office, including a congressman. After reviewing these qualities, we looked at the candidacy and campaign prom-ises of Jesus, who is our King of kings. The scripture passage was Luke 1:26-33, 38, though we also retraced the history of the mes-sianic hope from 2 Samuel through the Prophets. This sermon allowed us to examine the kind of king Jesus was as he walked this earth, and the kind of king he is today.

I offer these ideas merely to prompt your own creativity as you consider fresh ways to approach Advent—and help your congre-gation to prepare for, and fully understand the significance of, Christmas.

One final word about Christmas Eve itself. At Church of the Resurrection, as I mentioned earlier in the book, we have found that Christmas Eve is a night when the unchurched will come to worship. Some churches turn these services over primarily to their music department. Some invite guest preachers or associate pastors to preach on this night. I have always felt this was the one night I needed to preach, and to preach a very compelling and powerful sermon outlining the significance of Christmas for the lives of those present. I cannot overstate the importance of preparing and preaching an excellent sermon on Christmas Eve. The music and candlelighting alone will carry a service and allow it to be moving to those participating. But a sermon offering peace, hope, joy, and love to those who attend—helping them truly understand their need for God's gift in Jesus Christ, their need for Christmas—will allow this night to become not merely moving, but life-changing.

My Christmas Eve sermons are usually very simple—without a lot of teaching—but they are filled with stories that illustrate the difference the birth, life, death, and resurrection of Jesus make in the lives of real people. It is here that your passion, conviction, and prayerful preparation can have a powerful impact on those in attendance.

CHAPTER THIRTEEN

RETHINKING "PROPHETIC" PREACHING

Y ou have had hints, throughout this book, of sermons I have given that were a bit challenging or difficult to preach, or that met with some opposition. There are times when God calls us to preach a timely and important word to our people—a word that is challenging and which may be difficult to receive. In seminary we called this "prophetic preaching." We looked to the Old Testament prophets as our example—they were courageous and willing to speak the hard words of criticism as they preached against the sins of injustice, unfaithfulness, and idolatry that had infiltrated God's people in their day.

Having sought to faithfully deliver those kinds of messages with some degree of regularity at Church of the Resurrection, I would like to offer some insights I have gained, through both my successes and failures, in this area. My hope is that what I have learned may help you as you seek, in the words of Reinhold

Niebuhr, not only to "comfort the afflicted" but to "afflict the comfortable."

A Changing Influence

I have watched pastors, who were quite proud of their "prophetic ministry," drive churches right into the ground. Or, if they did not drive the church into the ground, they succeeded in driving away everyone who disagreed with them and only attracting like-minded people to the church (often difficult-to-find, like-minded people!). What they did not manage to do, unfortunately, was to actually influence people to change.

One of the questions we have to ask as we're called to preach about issues that are unpopular or controversial is: Is our aim to proudly, perhaps even arrogantly, shout out our position, or is it to actually influence people to consider making this position their own? By the way I've written the question, I am leading you to my conclusion: that our aim is to influence others to consider changing their views when their views would seem to be in conflict with what the scripture teaches.

If we agree about this, the next question we must ask when preaching on difficult topics is, "What is the most effective way to influence people to reconsider their own views and to move them to adopt a more biblical view?"

Show Honor and Respect

I have, at times, come right out in a sermon with what I believe is the biblical mandate, and preached it with both conviction and, unfortunately, a bit of self-righteousness or smugness. My approach never accomplished what I hoped it would—it did not move people with entrenched opinions to reconsider. I received plenty of kudos from those who already agreed with me, but only angered those who did not. This is not prophetic preaching, and it does not please God. It does not please God because the preacher (in this case me!) squandered an opportunity to make a real difference, and instead drove people even farther away from the position God was seeking to lead them toward. God isn't interested in whether you are right about a particular issue. God is interested in whether you do your job as a preacher, which is to help other people discover God's ways. Here's what I have learned over the years. The best way to influence and persuade others is not to alienate and irritate them, but to honor them and respect their positions, and then to respectfully and humbly offer an alternative position. Allow me to share my experience in preaching a series of sermons I referred to earlier entitled, "Christianity and the Controversial Issues of Our Time." This was a series of sermons that could have been disastrous if handled the wrong way. But it ended up being a tremendous success, not only in reaching and attracting a large number of new people, but also in influencing people to rethink their entrenched views on very difficult issues.

My underlying assumption in preaching this series of sermons was that controversial issues are controversial precisely because thinking Christians can reach opposite conclusions about the issues. If the issues were simple and the conclusion easily drawn, they would not be controversial. With this in mind, I prepared each sermon just as I had been required to prepare for debates in high school—I studied both sides of an issue with the goal of being able to win a debate regardless of whether I took the affirmative or the negative side of the argument. In other words, if I was going to preach successfully on a controversial topic, I needed to be able to understand and fairly articulate both sides of the issue.

Only after I could do this was I in a position to bring my own interpretation of the scripture, as it related to the particular issue, to bear. I had to be honest about the weaknesses of my argument, and I needed to be willing to change my own views as I considered the arguments.

My approach in presenting these sermons was to begin by making the strongest possible case for the view I would not ultimately ascribe to. I would in every case try to give proponents of this view the benefit of the doubt. I would attribute to them the highest possible motives. By the time I was done presenting the first position on any of the controversial issues, I wanted anyone who held that position to say, "Adam has been more than fair in representing my viewpoint, and he treated me and my viewpoint with respect." People often told me after these sermons that I did a far better job articulating their position than they could have done themselves. After this I presented the opposite view, not as my own, but as an objective presenter—again making the strongest case possible for this view and treating with respect those who held such views. My hope at this juncture in the sermon was simply to help people on both sides of the debate to understand and view each other with respect. I sought to model this approach for them.

Finally, I would try to bring my own thought processes to bear on the topic. I sought to demonstrate compassion for those on the opposite side of the issue, my own tentativeness if I was not completely certain myself, and then my final conclusion of what I felt was the position most in keeping with what I could understand of God's will as revealed in scripture and in the person of Jesus Christ.

Here's what I found: Some people told me, "Your conclusion was different from mine, but you have given me a lot to think about. I'll keep thinking about this." On many occasions, especially related to the death penalty, euthanasia, and abortion, people said, "I came here today with strong opinions in one direction, and I am leaving seriously reconsidering my views. You changed my mind today."

At the end of the day, I believe that is what effective prophetic preaching is supposed to do: to actually affect the people who most need to hear it. It is meant to move them to change—to reconsider their life or their views. If you can—with humility, respect, and great love—offer a challenging word, you have the incredible potential of actually changing the hearts and minds of your hearers.

If you have offered the difficult words with humility, respect, and love, and people are upset with you and choose to walk out on your sermons (as I have had happen on numerous occasions), so be it. You cannot avoid preaching on difficult subjects just because you don't want to lose members. I have received well over one hundred e-mails and letters during the last twelve years from people who disagreed with something I said in a sermon. Their words have sometimes hurt. But if I have been wise and caring in how I approach a difficult issue about which I feel God has called the church to speak, then I will accept the fact that some will occasionally turn away as a result of my sermons. But if *by my approach* I have alienated people and turned them away from the church and from the position I feel God has called me to preach, then I have failed.

One last word. I recently forgot my own advice here. On the one-year anniversary of September 11, I preached a sermon to my congregation that was stirred by my own growing conviction that as a nation we were too quickly headed for war with Iraq. I was not persuaded that we had met the criteria of just war. While 68 percent of the American people were in favor of moving forward, I was feeling increasingly convicted that I needed to challenge our assumptions about this. The first half of my sermon that day dealt with the kind of pastoral concerns that needed to be dealt with on the one-year anniversary of this terrible tragedy. But I devoted the second half of the sermon to the issue of our continuing war on terrorism, and specifically the prospects of war with Iraq.

As I look at that sermon I continue to feel the basic position I took in the sermon was biblical and prompted by the Holy Spirit. Unfortunately, what I did not do was respect and recognize the feelings and rationale of those who felt we were justified in going to war. Instead I simply let loose with my own understanding of God's will. The result was that I irritated a lot of folks I really had hoped to influence. In other words, I had failed to accomplish the one thing I most wanted to do that day—because I forgot the lessons I've just tried to teach you.

In the end this is the question when it comes to preaching on difficult issues: Do you want to irritate or influence your congregation?

CHAPTER FOURTEEN

WEDDINGS AND FUNERALS

If you are a seminary student, or just beginning your ministry, this chapter will be one of the most important in the entire book, and in it I will offer you some insights that I learned by trial and error through actually officiating at hundreds of weddings and funerals. If you are a seasoned pastor and effective at both weddings and funerals, most of what I am about to share you are likely already doing. But even for you I hope there may be one or two ideas or insights that spark your own creativity.

Weddings

Inconvenience or Opportunity?

I have known two kinds of seasoned pastors when it comes to weddings: The first are those who see weddings as an inconvenience, especially when they are done for unchurched persons looking for a "church wedding." In the same camp but slightly less pessimistic are those who see weddings simply as an opportunity to pick up a little extra cash. Many pastors, if they are honest, would admit to such feelings about weddings. It is easy to understand how this happens. Sometimes the pastor feels taken advantage of by a couple, treated as a hired hand, or a couple forget to provide an honorarium, or, often, a couple are married in the church and never seen again. A pastor can easily say, "Why should I give up five to ten hours of my life, especially my weekend evenings, for this ministry?"

But there is a second kind of pastor who looks at weddings as a huge opportunity to minister not only with a couple at one of the most significant moments in their lives, but also with a whole room full of their friends who are coming to church, and who are a captive audience to minister to. Pastors of this type recognize the leverage and influence they have over this couple during premarital counseling and take seriously the challenge to become the pastor for this man and woman. The pastor earnestly seeks to teach the couple about the importance of faith in a marriage. Such pastors demonstrate love to these couples and their friends, they pray for these couples, and they invest the time it takes to prepare for a wedding ceremony that is personal, beautiful, and inspired. These pastors find joy in this ministry—they love being the one person who looks in the eyes of the couple as they stand before God sharing in the vows of marriage, they love placing their hands on this couple as they pray over them following the taking of the vows—ordaining them to the ministry of Christian marriage, and they are grateful for the opportunity to be a physical reminder of the presence of Christ at the wedding. These pastors report that a significant number of people join their churches as a result of their wedding ministry.

Which pastor are you? If you are the former, I understand. I have occasionally felt that way—especially during seasons when I was feeling burned out and had little time for my family. But at times like those I force myself to remember the truths that inspire the latter kind of pastor, and I choose to be the latter kind of pastor. Both as an associate pastor who did many weddings, and for the last twelve years as the pastor of the Church of the Resurrection, I have sought to represent Christ—to embody his love and presence—to more than two hundred couples whose weddings I performed, and almost all of them ended up joining the church. More than that, hundreds of people who have joined the Church of the Resurrection said, "My first exposure to this church was when I came to a wedding you preached."

I know some of you are skeptical about this. I have talked with many pastors who have told me, "I never see the couple again. I never see anyone join the church as a result of my ministry at weddings. I only feel used when performing weddings." What I am about to share with you are the things I do in preparation for weddings and in the officiating of the actual service itself. I believe that when pastors do these things, weddings become tremendous opportunities for profound ministry, evangelism, and outreach. One last word before delving into the mechanics of weddings: I look at my ministry of weddings through the lens of the purpose of the church and my purpose as a pastor. My purpose is to do all I can to "build a Christian community where nonreligious and nominally religious people are becoming deeply committed Christians." This is the way I approach my ministry at weddings.

Premarital Counseling

Today we have a premarital counseling course that is offered multiple times throughout the year. It is four weeks long and is led by a Christian psychologist on our staff, except for the last session, on the spiritual dimension of marriage, which is taught by one of our pastors. Couples are required to take this course or they cannot be married in our church. As I mentioned earlier in the book, we also give couples a set of my sermons on "Biblical Perspectives on Love, Marriage, and Sex," building in the cost of these tapes to the fees charged for the wedding. (Note: A study based on these sermons will be published in 2004. The actual video- and audiotapes of the sermons themselves are available from the church's Web site at www.cor.org.) Following this course I meet one time with the couple. When we were a smaller church, however, I did all the premarital counseling with couples, meeting with them three or four times prior to the wedding.

There are many excellent books and guides to what should take place in premarital counseling. I commend these to your reading as you determine what you will do in your premarital counseling sessions. What I would like to mention here is what is not usually suggested in those books. First, prior to meeting with a couple I pray for them and ask God to use me to minister to and bless them. As I welcome the couple into my office, my aim is to reflect the love of Christ to them. Most couples have never been in a pastor's office—they are a little apprehensive and are not exactly sure what to expect. I try to put them at ease. And I always tell them, with genuine enthusiasm, how honored and excited I am to officiate at their wedding. I thank them for the privilege of doing so. My aim is to love this couple and to bless them by being excited with and for them.

I always open and close my premarital counseling sessions with prayer. Few adults ever have another adult pray out loud for them. This is especially true of the unchurched. I pray for God's blessings upon the couple, and that God would use me to prepare them for a lifetime of love and ministry to one another. At the close of each session I have the couples join me in holding hands and, based on the things we spoke of during the session, I pray a very specific prayer for them.

At some point during the premarital counseling, usually on the first session (this is still part of what I do even though I just meet with couples one time), I ask the man and woman to tell me their story—and specifically when and how they met, their first date, how they came to fall in love. Then I ask them each in turn to tell me what it is they treasure about the other person—what they see in their future spouse that causes them to want to marry this person. All this time I am taking copious notes, as this information is what I will use to personalize the service later on. Most couples love to talk about these things, and your ministry of listening to them is important.

I ask each partner to write a two-page letter to me answering these questions they have just answered in my office: "Why do you want to marry this person? What is it about them you most appreciate or love?" This gives them more time to reflect on their answers, and the written answers again provide material to help me in the preparation of their wedding ceremony. When I did all the premarital counseling, the last session was always set aside to talk about the spiritual dimension of marriage and then to plan the actual ceremony. Today this is the primary focus of the one session I have with the couple. If either or both of the partners are not practicing Christians, this is a tremendous opportunity to share the faith with them in a nonthreatening and pastoral way.

I talk with them about the biblical concept of covenant, and marriage as a ministry or calling in which we are expected to act as a companion and helper to this person, and in which we are asked to love them with Christ's love, and to live a life of faith toward the other person. I typically will use Colossians 3:12-17 as a description of the expectations God has for us in marriage:

> As God's chosen ones, holy and beloved, clothe yourselves with compassion, kindness, humility, meekness, and patience. Bear with one another and, if anyone has a complaint against another, forgive each other; just as the Lord has forgiven you, so you also must forgive. Above all, clothe yourselves with love, which binds everything together in perfect harmony. And let the peace of Christ rule in your hearts, to which indeed you were called in the one body. And be thankful. Let the word of Christ dwell in you richly; teach and admonish one another in all wisdom; and with gratitude in your hearts sing psalms, hymns, and spiritual songs to God. And whatever you do, in word or deed, do everything in the name of the Lord Jesus, giving thanks to God the Father through him.

I share with the couple experiences from my own marriage and the ways my wife and I live out this passage toward one another. I encourage them to pray for one another and with one another.

And I plead with them to be involved together in church, sharing with them how this influences a relationship.

Finally I invite the couple to sit by my desk as I put together a draft of their actual wedding ceremony. We tell couples when they reserve their wedding date that the pastor is responsible for the actual wedding service itself and all its content, and that any changes to that ceremony must be approved by the pastor. This helps me to guide the couple through the process. I let them know that, having done a couple hundred weddings, I have had the opportunity to see things that work and things that do not work so well in a wedding, and that my aim is to help them have the most beautiful wedding possible. We then begin to talk about the ceremony. I walk them through the standard ceremony we use, which at this time I have pulled up on my computer screen. I then ask them about the songs they intend to use in the wedding (our wedding policies, which they received when reserving the date for the wedding, outline that songs should be appropriate for a service of worship, and that our musicians are happy to help couples with choosing music if they need help). We try not to be too restrictive when it comes to music that is chosen. I ask if there are any special elements they want to include in the ceremony that may not be part of the standard service. I tell the couple that the homily is where their service will be most personal. I let them know that my aim in the homily is to offer an eight- or nine-minute message that tells the story of their love for each other, and then teaches the congregation what marriage is meant to be from the biblical perspective—some of the same things I have just shared with them in the session.

I will then take all the information just gained, type the songs in the appropriate places and add any other elements that may not be included in the standard service, and then I print off a copy of the service—my personal "cheat sheet," which includes their names in all the appropriate places. I have typed the entire wedding ceremony into my computer so that I can print off this complete copy of the service, to help me so I don't slip during the ceremony, but also to assist all others who are playing a part in the ceremony—the coordinator, the musicians, and the scripture readers. We end this session by praying together once again, and then I express once more my excitement for the couple.

Rehearsal

We schedule all rehearsals at 5:00 on the evening before the wedding. This allows me to have the rest of the evening with my family while allowing the couple to get to dinner relatively early. Our rehearsals last about forty-five minutes. I try, from the outset, to clearly be in charge of the rehearsal. The worst rehearsals I have ever attended occurred when I was co-officiating at weddings and the lead pastors did not take charge. The rehearsals were unpleasant and chaotic. You, as pastor, are in charge of this wedding ceremony—you are the expert and have done this many times. The couple, and even the parents of the couple, have limited experience planning a wedding. If you take charge, they will not. (This may sound a bit harsh—I don't mean it to be so.) You can take charge in a loving and caring way that doesn't offend, and this is what I seek to do.

I begin the rehearsal promptly at 5:00 P.M., inviting the wedding party to gather at the front of the church. I introduce myself and tell them how excited the church is to be hosting this wedding and how honored I am to be officiating. I introduce them to our wedding coordinator and explain that she is there to minister to them and bless them and to help the wedding go as planned. I introduce them to the organist. And then I ask the wedding party to join me in praying for the bride and groom.

I am recounting all these details, probably far more than you want, to make a point—namely, that your spirit, attitude, enthusiasm, love, and prayers—all are means of ministering with this couple and their family and helping them experience the love of Christ through you in such a way that they will want to return to the church. This may be the first time that some in the wedding party have even been "up close and personal" with a pastor.

We walk through the wedding ceremony once completely, and then a second time just through the processional and introduction to the service. I end the rehearsal by taking the couple aside and praying for them once more, letting them know that my wife and I will be praying for them that night before we go to bed.

The Ceremony

I will not here describe the entire wedding ceremony and the various do's and don'ts of the service. But I do want to describe the homily itself. As I mentioned above, the homily is eight to nine minutes in length. I begin by describing how the couple first met, hoping there is some lighthearted part of the story that will make the congregation chuckle. I then describe their first date, their courtship, and their engagement. Next I say something like this: "I asked each of you to tell me what it is that you treasure about the other—why you want to marry this person. I'd like to share a bit of this with your friends and family." This is a tender point in the ceremony. It also serves to draw all the guests into the homily. Next I transition to the meaning of this thing they are about to do—what God's intention is and what it takes to have a successful marriage. This is an opportunity to subtly and tactfully talk about the importance of faith in a successful marriage. Finally, I will close the homily with a story of a successful marriage— a story that is moving and describes the nature of the love that God is calling us to. Finally I make the transition to the vows.

It is amazing how much impact these eight or nine minutes can have in the ceremony. If done with love and compassion, it will speak volumes not only to the couple, but to the guests as well. It is seldom that at least some guests at weddings held at our church don't end up visiting and ultimately joining our church.

One last note: An excellent wedding, including premarital counseling, will require a minimum of eight to ten hours of time.

Funerals

There is generally no time your ministry is more important to an individual or family than when a loved one dies. And if the individual or family is unchurched, there is no time when you will have a greater opportunity for building a relationship with the family that ultimately may lead to their coming to faith. As an associate pastor, and for the first four years of my ministry as senior pastor at Church of the Resurrection, I jumped at the opportunity to perform funerals for unchurched persons, especially if they lived within a reasonable distance of the church. If they did not, I encouraged the funeral home to find a pastor closer to their home to increase the likelihood of a continuing ministry relationship following the funeral. Today our associates do most of the funerals at the church—I officiate at about twelve per year, and I tend to focus on the more tragic losses.

Initial Visit

Like an excellent wedding, an excellent funeral, if the interment is nearby, will generally take at least ten hours. This includes going to the home immediately following the death of the loved one, simply to comfort and pray and give guidance regarding the next steps for making funeral arrangements. If the death was a tragedy, a pastor may stay for an hour or two at this time. Before leaving, a time is set for the pastor to return and meet with the immediate family to begin preparing for the funeral.

Subsequent Visit

This subsequent visit should be two days before the funeral if possible. I will usually go to the home of the family, taking with me notepaper, a pen, and a Bible. I begin once more with prayer, and then share with the family that my aim is to help them celebrate their loved one's life. I share with the closest family my preference that rather than having others stand to speak during the service, I would like to have them write down their comments, and I will incorporate them into one complete eulogy. I explain that by doing this I can better help them celebrate their loved one's life and keep the service an appropriate length, with the right feel. I try to suggest this gently and with love. If they continue to insist on having others share at the service, I ask that it be limited to two people and that these people prepare their comments in writing, no more than three or four minutes each, and fax or e-mail these to me in advance.

Why am I so restrictive on this point? Because the worst funerals I have ever attended were those where friends and family were invited to speak. They will often feel the need to preach, or to begin speaking about the role God played in "taking" their loved one, or what God's plans were in "calling them home." This kind of talk is fine when the decedent is elderly, but when the death was tragic, such talk turns God into the cause of their death. In addition, people who stand to speak often will break down, and when they break down emotionally it works against the design of the service, which is to begin bringing healing and hope. On occasion someone will come to the microphone and they will simply say very inappropriate things. And from time to time I have seen people talk for fifteen minutes or more.

As pastors we are, once again, called upon to be the experts in planning and leading funeral services. Most people have only been to a handful of services, and perhaps only helped plan one. When they are grieving they are usually not best able to think clearly about the service itself. I believe that if I know a way to help the service flow well, accomplish the greatest possible good, and help the service to be done with excellence, it is important that I share this with the family.

So, I will tell them that my aim is to write down all the things they will share with me on this day about their loved one. I will also ask if their loved one had any letters, a journal, or any papers or poems that they had written. I will invite anyone that was interested in sharing something—a friend or coworker or family member—to send me an e-mail or fax and I will include what they said and attribute their comments to this person. During this time I will sit with the family for an hour to an hour and a half, just taking notes and listening. I'll ask for any humorous stories they might be able to share with me as well. I will often ask to see the bedroom or some other personal space that was a favorite of the deceased—the colors of their room, the pictures hanging on their wall—all give me a sense of the individual. I will also ask the family if I can see any photos of the deceased, hoping they will let me take a photo home to look at as I prepare the eulogy and homily. I will end by sharing words of scripture offering comfort and hope and then praying with the family.

Drafting the Service

I will then spend three to four hours in study, looking over my notes, considering scriptures that might speak to the deceased's life or offer hope and comfort to the family, and then drafting the funeral service and homily. Unless the family has strong feelings about music, I will generally suggest hymns and special music based on my review of the notes I have taken regarding their loved one and the flow of the service. I usually choose the scriptures, though I always ask if their loved one had any favorites.

Again, our task is to help plan excellent funeral services. Most families do not know what music is available for times like this, so they go back to the handful of hymns they have heard at other funerals: "In the Garden," "Amazing Grace," "How Great Thou Art." These are fine, and I will gladly use them if they are important to the family, but it may be that I know of other hymns that would be significant, and tie in well to their loved one's life, that the family does not know or think of at this time. The same is true of special music. As pastors we should be familiar with songs for a variety of funerals that our people will not know of. If we simply ask for their selections we will likely hear of songs like, "The Wind Beneath My Wings" or other popular songs they have heard at other funerals. Again, these may be fine, but you should keep in mind other choices of wonderful music they may not be aware of. One suggestion: If the family has a particular secular song that they want to use, I will generally use it, but I will listen to the song over and over and see if there is some way to tie it into the homily.

As is the case with weddings, I have a service in my computer that I start with as the basic foundation for each funeral. Saving it as a new document, I change the name of the deceased and then rebuild the service based upon the wishes of the family and the work that I have done. The finished product is then a complete service with every word and prayer, except for my homily, which will be a separate document. I copy the service and give it to the musicians, the funeral director, and anyone else who needs it. I will also provide copies to the family after the service.

When it comes to the homily itself, I generally combine the eulogy and homily, in much the same way that I shared personal stories about couples before moving to the theological significance of marriage in the wedding ceremony. I will preach for about fifteen to twenty minutes, depending on the situation. My sermons are generally a bit longer if the death was untimely or tragic.

The Homily

The sermon begins with stories about the deceased—stories and descriptions of this individual that everyone will recognize, and that will bring a smile to their faces, a nod of their heads, or occasionally a laugh. Laughter is such an important element to introduce into the service—it promotes healing and helps lift the hearts of those present. But here, too, less is more. One or two humorous anecdotes will be plenty. Following these personal stories and celebration of the individual's life, I will move to a short homily based on scriptures that were anchored in the individual's life. The point of the homily is to offer encouragement, to paint a picture of God's grace and love, and to lift up the Christian understanding of resurrection and hope.

When you are preaching on the untimely death of an individual, it is important that you understand and deal with the questions that are running through the minds of those sitting in the pews. I guarantee you, they are struggling with their faith. Many are angry and disappointed with God for "taking" their friend. Some, who already had questions of faith, are now convinced there is no God. If you are aware of this and do not address it in your homily, you have done a great disservice to these people and missed an opportunity for ministry that is profound. You must deal with the problem of evil and suffering at this funeral. These people need to know how to reconcile belief in a God they can turn to at this time, with a painful and unthinkable tragedy that seems wholly inconsistent with that kind of God. If you can help them through this, you will have done significant ministry in this service of worship.

As a result of these tragic funerals, where we have openly dealt with the hard issues and questions people are wrestling with, we have seen hundreds of people join the church. But I am amazed at how many times pastors do not deal with these questions at funerals.

The ideal length of a funeral is forty-five minutes in today's culture. An hour is the outer limit. A graveside service will generally be only five or ten minutes in length. Here I will generally tell the story of God's forming of Adam from the dust of the earth and how he did not become a human being until God breathed into him a spirit. I remind them that our bodies came from the dust, but our spirit from the Lord, to whence we return. I will read the Twenty-third Psalm, and often either Charles Wesley's poem/hymn, "If Death My Friend and Me Divide" (#656 in *The United Methodist Hymnal*) or Natalie Sleeth's poem/hymn "Hymn of Promise" (#707 in *The United Methodist Hymnal*). Here, if there is only a small gathering, I may invite persons to share if they like, and then we have one final prayer of committal. I generally drive to the cemetery so that I can leave immediately following the service.

Follow-Up Care

Obviously, the funeral is just the first step in ministry—follow-up pastoral care is essential in good ministry with families following a death, especially after a tragic death.

Weddings and funerals are among the greatest opportunities for you to preach the good news at a time when people are most open to receiving it. It is a special honor to be a part of people's lives at times like this. If you approach them as such, filled with prayer and the desire to represent Christ, amazing things can happen through your ministry and preaching at weddings and funerals.

CHAPTER FIFTEEN

WHAT TO
DO IF . . .

Throughout this book I've been trying to offer pointers and concrete ideas for preaching—ideas that may not have been included as part of the standard seminary curriculum. But in this chapter I'd like to cover a few things that I am pretty sure your seminary professors didn't teach you!

Because of the size of our congregation and the sheer number of services, we tend to experience things every few years that most pastors might experience only once or twice in a lifetime. As a result, we have had to develop systems or responses to some of these things. Following are a few of the more unusual, difficult, or humorous things that have happened while I was preaching, along with what I've learned about how to respond.

Fire Alarms

One Sunday evening in the cold of winter, at the beginning of my sermon at our 5:00 service, one of the teens in our church thought it would be interesting to pull the fire alarm.

Unfortunately, no one could get the system to shut down, nor could they find the pull station that had been activated. Ours is a modern alarm complete with strobe lights, sirens, and a woman's voice that repeatedly says, "There has been a fire reported in the building. Please exit the building."

Well, we were pretty confident there was no fire, but we needed to take every precaution. I asked our members to take their coats and calmly make their way outside. There appeared to be no imminent danger of fire near the sanctuary, and the children's staff reported the kids were okay. I asked parents to pick up their children and meet on the lawn. If the building was going to burn down, they would want to see it. If not, we would have the most memorable worship service they had ever had here and one they would tell their friends about. I shared that I would offer an abbreviated version of my sermon, then we would take an offering and pray.

Amazingly, most of the people did stay for the service in the cold outside. I stood on a table to lead the rest of the service. We prayed for the firefighters, who by this time were searching the building, and thanked God for them. I talked about the people around the world who have no buildings to worship in, and the sacrifices people make to serve God, and that our standing in the cold was a witness to our faith. I shared a shortened version of my sermon. The ushers stood by the parking lot so people could leave their offerings with them as they left. And we ended by giving thanks for God's blessings and that our building was safe. People still talk about that night—what seemed a frustrating curse turned into a remarkable blessing.

Medical Emergencies

Several times each year we will have some kind of medical emergency during worship. We have a team of people who are trained to administer CPR and other first aid to someone in need. They have special name badges and reserved seats in the sanctuary so our staff and ushers know where to find them. But what do you as the preacher do when there is a medical emergency in the middle of your sermon in the sanctuary itself? Here's what we did in a recent situation. I had just begun preaching when one of our members in the balcony collapsed. I did not know what had happened at first, but soon the cardiac arrest response team (CART) were all running to the balcony. 911 was immediately called and an ambulance had been dispatched. I said to the congregation, "There appears to be a medical emergency in the balcony. In a moment I am going to go and check on this person and pray for them. Though I don't know what has happened, or who is ill, let's pause for a moment and together as God's people pray for our brother or sister. Following this I'll ask our musicians to play softly, and invite you to remain in your seats until we receive word on what is happening." I then led our congregation in prayer for the ill person. This prayer gave the organist time to get to her seat and have some music picked out that was gentle and calming. I quickly made my way to the balcony and prayed with one of our men who had fainted. He had since come to and the medical workers had arrived. I returned to the pulpit and asked once more that we pray for the medical workers as well as for our member.

I then had two choices: dismiss the service or keep going on. I said, "I believe if it were me who was ill, I would want the service to continue. I believe our brother will be okay. While the medical team is preparing to take him out, I'll share with you an abbreviated version of the sermon." This actually seemed to have a calming influence on the congregation and on those who were caring for the man in the balcony. The service ended, our people felt we had done the right thing and handled it with care, and our member who was taken to the hospital was fine. His blood sugar was a bit low, and he was easily able to adjust this and has been fine ever since.

As a general rule then, when there is a medical emergency always stop and pray for the one needing help, then pardon yourself from the service long enough to go and pray with this person and find out how he or she is doing. Return and lead the rest of the service, sending one of your leaders to be with the person at the hospital.

Bomb Threats

I hope this never happens to you, but it did happen to us. On the Sunday afternoon following September 11, 2001, someone called 911 and reported that there was a bomb in our building. This was about an hour and a half prior to our next worship service—our 5:00 P.M. service. We were expecting over two thousand people in attendance that night. We locked down the building and gathered all those who had been in the building so the police could question them. The fire department and police came and searched the building. Our worship team gathered outside with their guitars and led people in singing as they approached. Finally, at 4:30 P.M. the police and fire departments said they had done all they could do. They said the voice on the call to 911 sounded like a teen, but they could not be sure. As near as they could tell, there was no bomb and this was a hoax, like several others that had been called in the days following September 11. They would remain throughout the worship service but could not guarantee anyone's safety.

What do you do? The emotions were particularly frayed given the attack on the World Trade Center and Pentagon earlier in the week. We had 2,200 people show up for worship, and I began the service by telling the congregation exactly what had happened. I said, "The police and fire department believe this was a hoax but cannot guarantee that. If you would feel more comfortable going home tonight, please know I understand. You can pick up a copy of the sermon later this week. But as for me, I feel comfortable staying here. I can't tell you what to do, however. During the greeting time, if you would like to quietly slip out, please know this is okay." About a dozen of the people there that night slipped out, the rest stayed and felt a resolve and determination not to allow threats to keep them from worshiping the Lord. It ended up being the most powerful of the worship services that day.

Was this the right thing to do? It is hard to say. There are times you take the very best information you can, and every precaution possible, you make an informed decision, you share the information with the congregation and let them make their own decision. I can honestly say I was uncertain what the right course of action was that evening. I feel a great responsibility for the safety of our congregation. At the same time I did not want someone who irresponsibly called in a hoax to keep this congregation from finding the healing and hope it so desperately needed in the wake of the terrorist attack on America.

Other Mishaps

Okay, let's talk about a few of the more lighthearted things that can happen during worship.

During a wedding I was officiating, the young son of the bride, who was himself a groomsman standing on the chancel, began to vomit during the middle of the homily. Quickly one of the other groomsmen took him offstage and to the bathroom. We didn't draw any attention to this. The video of the wedding has, however, become a treasured family heirloom!

On Candlelight Christmas Eve, at the climax of the service we turn off all the lights and a child brings a lone lit candle down the aisle with her family in order to light the Christ Candle. There is not another light in the sanctuary on at this time. Several years ago the little girl came to the Christ candle and I looked at her and at her candle and said, "Okay, go ahead," meaning, go ahead and light the Christ candle. She proceeded to do what children are supposed to do when a candle is in front of them and an adult says, "Okay, go ahead." She blew the candle out! We were all standing in the dark wondering what to do next. Fortunately, we had a lighter hidden near the altar just in case something like this should happen. The lesson: Always be prepared!

What do you do when you go to the pulpit and you can't find your sermon manuscript because the song leader picked it up with his music books? You have two choices: You can draw attention to the situation by frantically trying to find your manuscript. Or you can take a deep breath, pretend the manuscript is there, and do the best job you can without it.

Along this line, there is much to be learned from Olympic figure skaters. When they make a mistake, they don't stop, draw attention to the mistake, and then try to start their routine all over. When possible, they incorporate the mistake into their routine so that the audience isn't sure whether it was really a mistake, or part of the performance—only the judges know the truth. Or, if the mistake is serious, they just get up and keep going, pretending it never happened. In preaching and in leading worship the best pastors and worship leaders don't miss a beat when something goes wrong. They don't draw attention to the mistake—they act as though this is part of the plan.

The exception is where the mistake can actually illustrate some spiritual truth. In a recent wedding the couple could not get the unity candle lit—the symbolism of this was not good—so I stepped over and pulled the wick of the unity candle up a bit, and tilted it at an angle so the couple could light it. It would have been fine to have gone on and not said another word about this. But there was also a teaching moment here at the end of the service. As I was presenting the couple I took a moment to say, "In lighting your unity candle there is a great lesson: In marriage things don't always go according to plan. But if you don't give up, if you are willing to persevere, things usually work out just fine in the end." This took what seemed like an embarrassing moment and transformed it into a memorable and important part of the wedding.

We've had many interesting challenges with regard to sound issues. One Sunday the sound system went out at the beginning of worship. In many sanctuaries this wouldn't be a terrible problem, but in a sanctuary that seats sixteen hundred people it is a bit more problematic. We learned two things on that morning. First, always have a plan for rigging a backup sound system quickly. Our sound guys are amazing, and by the end of the service they had a backup sound system cannibalized from our youth room and we were good to go. That still left me shouting throughout the first service. Since that time we have had a backup system instantly available that will provide us with at least a few microphones to allow worship to go on.

On several occasions my wireless lavalier microphone has gone down during worship, usually because of a bad battery. We always have a handheld wireless microphone under the pulpit that I can grab, and in the time it takes to turn it on, most of our congregation does not even realize what has happened.

You likely have a host of your own stories to tell. The key thing is to keep your cool, to not overreact or draw excessive attention to the surprise, and to keep moving on. Sometimes the mishaps are wonderful opportunities in disguise.

CHAPTER SIXTEEN

A FINAL WORD
TO PREACHERS

Well, we've come to the end of our discussion about preaching, but there are a few things yet to share with you. I offer these miscellaneous thoughts as a final bit of encouragement and help as you continue in your work of preaching the gospel.

The first is a story: One year on Christmas Eve as I was on my way to the church for the first of six candlelight services, I began to pray. Instantly I heard God speak to me—not in an audible voice but in such a startling and overwhelming thought that it stopped me cold. Here's what I heard God say, "You didn't pray much this week, did you?" I was so startled and convicted that I spoke aloud and said, "O Lord, you are right! I was so busy preparing my sermon that I never stopped to seek your will, your help, your guidance. Forgive me Lord!" I felt this sense of panic as I walked into the building. Frantically I began doing what I should have been doing all week: I began praying, first as I walked through each section of chairs, asking God to bless those who would be seated in them, and then at the kneelers, as I sought to yield myself to God.

An hour later I got up to preach and the sermon was fine. It was well written. My presentation was okay. Yet I knew there was something missing. I had to work very hard to preach. My heart was heavy and I felt no joy in the delivery. So it went for the first three services. The comments after church were all positive and the services went well, but there was something missing. Just before I got up to preach the fourth service I felt God speaking to me again. This time I heard the Lord say, "I let you do the first three on your own power. Now I will show you what happens when you preach with the power of my Spirit." As I began to preach at that service, I felt the heaviness on my heart dissipate. I felt a power in my preaching. In the midst of the sermon something palpable happened to the congregation. You could hear a pin drop. The service was almost overwhelming. This continued throughout the rest of the evening's sermons. At the end of one of the last services my wife came to me—she had been present for the first service and now for one of these last three. She said, "What did you do to your sermon? It was so different from before." The truth is, it was exactly the same manuscript, exactly the same sermon—only this time it was preached with the power of the Holy Spirit.

My African American friends refer to this as "the Anointing." Given the choice of preaching with the anointing of the Holy Spirit or preaching in my own power, I choose the Spirit's power. But this anointing comes when we have spent adequate time in prayer, yielding to the Holy Spirit. I know some of you are left-brain people (I am one of those myself), and this idea of the "anointing" may seem a bit concocted. But this work of the Holy Spirit is real. When the Holy Spirit empowers our preaching, our sermons rise to a whole new level of effectiveness.

Okay, a second important idea: Pastors, you have to take care of yourself. There are times we get tired, run down, and burned out. And when we do, our entire congregation pays the price for it. The effectiveness of your preaching is directly related to whether you are taking care of yourself spiritually, physically, emotionally, and relationally. In the United Methodist Church every full-time pastor is granted four weeks vacation—take all of your vacation. Take your day off. Spend time reading, resting, and being renewed.

Sabbath is important for everyone, and if you do not take a day to rest, you are violating this important biblical principle.

Take seriously your devotional and prayer life. I was taught in seminary that I shouldn't blend my preaching preparation and my devotional life together. But I have found that when I approach my reading, research, and study time as part of my devotional and spiritual life, both are enriched. Start your time of study for your sermon with prayer, dedicating that time to God. Invite God to speak to you and to shape your heart as a result of this study.

Remember that every sermon you preach will not be a home run. I want each sermon to be a grand slam, out-of-the-parker, but it doesn't work that way. The greatest baseball players in the major leagues only get a hit one out of three times at bat! Some of your sermons will be extraordinary. Some will be average. Some will be sub-par. Our task is to do all we can to raise the sub-par sermons to averages, to raise the averages to above average, and to strive to hit a few more homers each year.

I think one in eight of my sermons are messages that I am most proud of. Six of the remaining seven range from average to above average. One in eight sermons is the kind I want to apologize for when I am finished preaching. And yes, I know that sometimes people tell us after those sub-par sermons, "That was one of your best sermons." But be careful in taking too much solace from those comments—sometimes they're just feeling sorry for us!

This brings us back to the Christmas Eve story. Ultimately it is the Holy Spirit who takes our feeble efforts each week and transforms them into experiences in which God speaks to his people. There are times when I have tried my best to listen to the Lord. I have studied and worked and prepared and I still felt like the sermon wasn't quite right. At those times my prayer sounds something like this, "Lord, I've done all I know to do. I prayed, inviting you to guide me. I studied and read and researched and diligently worked on this message. If you want something else said, now's the time to tell me, but I've done all I can do." When you've done your part, turn it over to God. You can rest knowing you did your best to hear from God.

If you are married, would you have your spouse read the next three paragraphs? I wrote these for her or him.

My wife attends our Saturday evening worship service and one of our services on Sunday morning. At the Saturday evening service she takes notes for her own benefit and to help me as well. When we get home on Saturday evenings I want to know what she thinks—sort of. I need her input: I need to know about places where she thinks I spent too much time, portions of the sermon that didn't make sense to her, and her overall impression. But I also need to hear what was good in the sermon. Her critique always helps me to improve the sermon. In this she is my partner. What she sometimes does not understand however is that my sermons are like children to me, or at least like works of art. I have a lot invested in them. I feel very personal about them. I need her to be gentle with criticism and to sprinkle it with praise. I need the criticism—what a blessing to have some way to improve the sermon before the next day when I preach it five more times. But coupled with this criticism, I need to hear that there was something valuable she found in the message. LaVon does an excellent job of this. Her words of encouragement give me confidence in the message. I know that her words of criticism are given in love and help me to improve the message.

Now, for most of you spouses, you won't have a chance to critique your mate's messages in time for them to change anything (unless you encourage them to rehearse with you each week prior to Sunday). So, here's a word of advice: Say something positive about your mate's message, and build her or his self-confidence. Don't share strong criticism in the first hour or so after he or she finishes preaching for the day. But sometime a day or so later, mention any suggestions you may have that might help him or her be a more effective preacher the next time.

Half the battle in becoming an effective preacher is gaining self-confidence. This is also true in sports and nearly any other endeavor. One of the most important things that LaVon has done for me over the years was to help me believe in myself—to help me believe that I could preach and that I had something important to say.

Okay, I am writing the following letter specifically to the leaders in your church. Would you mind passing this on to them?

Dear Church Leader,

I want to offer a word of encouragement to you regarding your pastor. The single most important thing your pastor will do every week for the over-all health of your church is preach excellent sermons. But a pastor will only preach excellent sermons when he or she has time to prepare. Sermon preparation includes extensive reading, prayer, Bible study, reflection, and writing. This will generally require about fifteen hours of uninterrupted time per week (some weeks a little less, some weeks a little more).

I believe you will see a direct correlation between the time you give your pastor to focus on sermon preparation and the quality of the sermons. I find I need to work at my home study, or sometimes at a library, in order to have the quiet time to prepare my sermons. Your pastor may find that to be true as well.

This may require that you help your congregation assume responsibility for freeing this time for your pastor. You may need to involve laity in doing some of the pastoral care needed during this fifteen hours, or you may need to change the expectations of your congregation regarding the times your pastor is available.

In addition to this weekly time, there is value in your pastor taking a bit of extra time throughout the year to plan out sermons in advance. You might ask him or her to let you borrow this book so you can read the section on sermon planning and the time that is required for this.

In addition, encourage your pastor and build up his or her self-confidence about preaching. The great athletes of our time work hard and have strong skills, but one of the most important things they cannot succeed without is self-confidence. Help build up your pastor. Let him or her know when something speaks to you in the sermon, and try to find something that speaks to you each week. Finally, provide funds for your pastor to be able to purchase books to add to his or her library that will help in preparing quality sermons. Also, make it possible for your pastor to travel to seminars on preaching, or simply to hear other excellent preachers. All of these things will be an investment in both your pastor's preaching and in the health of your church.

Blessings!

Adam Hamilton

Finally, preachers, I want to lift up three words that should define not only your preaching but your life. People can sense when these are not present, and your entire ministry will be ineffective without them. But when people see and experience these three things in you, they will listen to what you have to say. Here they are:

• Humility • Authenticity • Integrity

When it comes to integrity I am aware that I have not always practiced what I am preaching as I offer a sermon. In fact, the best sermons are often effective precisely because God was convicting me first. But once I have preached the sermon, I make it my aim to do what I have just challenged others to do.

On another note, take your work seriously, but don't take yourself so seriously. Laugh at yourself. Remember that you are simply the interpreter—people have come to hear from God. Don't be crushed by criticism, but don't become ruined by praise.

Thank you for taking the time to read this book. My prayer has been that it would bless those who read it, that it would stir in your mind creative new ideas and in your heart a renewed excitement about the wonderful and terrifying work of preaching. No other work has greater potential to bring healing, transformation, and hope to the world than the work of announcing peace, good news, salvation, and the reign of God!

How beautiful upon the mountains
    are the feet of the messenger who announces peace,
who brings good news,
    who announces salvation,
who says to Zion, "Your God reigns." (Isaiah 52:7)